UNTIL HE FIND IT

The George F. Dempster
Memorial Volume

BOOKS BY GEORGE F. DEMPSTER

LOVEST THOU ME?

TOUCHED BY A LOVING HAND

FINDING MEN FOR CHRIST

THE LOVE THAT WILL NOT LET ME GO

GEORGE F. DEMPSTER

UNTIL HE FIND IT

The Memorial Volume Edited and Introduced by Geoffrey R. King

HODDER AND STOUGHTON

FIRST PUBLISHED 1956
FIFTH IMPRESSION 1968

SBN 340 01839 9

Printed in Great Britain
for Hodder and Stoughton Ltd.,
St. Paul's House, Warwick Lane, London, E.C.4,
by Richard Clay (The Chaucer Press), Ltd.,
Bungay, Suffolk

TO DONALD

Whose love, in expression, eased the way Home.

M. T. D.

BY WAY OF INTRODUCTION

THIS little volume explains itself. It is his memorial book. In the main part, "The Work He Did", the first two chapters are the beginnings of his new book, which he was not able to finish. The other chapters were all in manuscript form, in his neat, clear handwriting, and include all the stories that are left. I have worked through them and arranged them, but they are very much as he left them, without material alteration. It has been for me a labour of love and a very great privilege. To have known him well, to have loved him and been loved by him, has been an enrichment beyond words.

GEOFFREY R. KING

On the return journey from Westcliff on June 22nd, 1955, to an empty house, my whole thought was concentrated on arrangements to be made; and the decision arrived at was that everything must be as my husband would have wished.

The church, George Lane Congregational, was chosen because the Rev. Wm. Hallett had been so unfailingly kind during the illness and crises, and also because it was large enough for all those who would wish to pay tribute.

God guided my thought to the Rev. Geoffrey King for the Address, who, when approached, needed much persuasion, in his humility. He came in spite of the fact that he was commencing a preaching flight round the world two days later, and proved a tower of strength. Will any who were present ever forget his words? There were no tears, for the whole theme was Victory and Love; and we praised God for a life of Service.

The publishers asked for the Address to be printed, and requested Mr. King to prepare a brief survey of my husband's life. These, with G. F. D.'s manuscripts prepared in response to many requests, but incomplete, are in this volume.

Mr. King readily responded, and I wish to place on record my warmest thanks for all his help and gracious understanding.

One must also speak of the help and co-operation of Mr. Leonard Cutts (Hodder & Stoughton) in this and in every volume from my husband's pen. But for his patient determination and persistence, I doubt if "Finding Men For Christ" would ever have been printed.

God be thanked for the life of George F. Dempster, always willingly obedient to the Master's call. May all who loved him endeavour so to live and serve that they may share in the Joy of the Morning!

MARY T. DEMPSTER

SYMPATHY

Could I tell that someone wanted
  Just the word that I could speak;
Could I know that I'd the message
  Hungry souls around me seek;
I would surely speak in accents
  True and tender, brave and strong;
I would tell the wondrous story,
  How One suffered much and long;
How He came to carry burdens
  That no other one could bear;
How He seeks each heart to enter,
  Every pang of pain to share.

Could I feel the lonely heartache
  Of the passer in the street;
Could I hear the sob of anguish
  In the breast of one I meet;
I would speak, whate'er it cost me;
  I would sing the song of cheer;
I would chase away the shadows,
  Strive to bring the Saviour near;
I would tell the world, far seeking
  For a balm to heal its woes,
That the Master still is speaking
  To the hearts whose need He knows.

"Come all ye who vainly labour,
  Take my yoke and learn of Me"—
Thus He speaks to all the weary,
  Yearning still to set them free.
Hearts there are around me aching
  For the comfort I can bring;

Souls there are about me longing
  For the sunshine I can fling;
Feet there are whose steps are weary;
  Eyes there are with tears grown dim,
Ever groping in the darkness;
  I should lead them up to Him.

For I know that men around me
  Feel a want they never tell.
Words I know that I have spoken,
  Pained or wounded where they fell.
I will speak in words more gentle,
  To the soul I chance to meet;
I will give to each one freely
  Smiles of sympathy, full sweet.
Since I know, my pace must slacken,
  I must step with greater care
Lest my careless feet be treading
  In the dust some jewel rare.

G. F. D.

CONTENTS

THE MAN HE WAS

THE MEMORIAL ADDRESS

delivered by the Rev. Geoffrey R. King at the Funeral Service on June 27th, 1955

I AM sure that you will all agree with me that it is a very sacred privilege to be here today. This was no ordinary man. The fact that so many of you have come, from such varied walks of life and from considerable distances, proves that we loved him and honoured him and that God has done us all good by him. Memories of this man of God both bless and burn. Every remembrance is refreshing; but he made us all ashamed. I think the challenge of what he was and did will never leave us.

I shall never forget when a friend sent me an autographed copy of "Finding Men for Christ" soon after Hodder & Stoughton had let it loose upon the world. I could not lay it down. I read on far into the night. I was in my second year of ministry in East London, and that book shattered me and yet upbuilt me. It was Harold Begbie all over again, but more so, and right up to date. For me, it was right on the district, too. Do you also recall the impress of that book the first time you read it?

Nor shall I ever forget the first time I saw him. I had imagined a big, brawny man, with massive voice and magnetic smile, a kind of bruiser, yet with rare beauty, a prize-fighter and preacher in one. The mind plays queer tricks, and I think I was associating him in my imagination with Jack Dempsey! I was amazed when I met him. That small, slight man, so insignificant, could not possibly be George Dempster. But then he turned. I found myself looking into a face so full of character as instantly to command respect and inspire confidence. Later I was to see something of that piercing look under those dark lashes that could, by sheer force of personality under the Spirit of God, quell wrongdoers and curb the passions of evil men. There is nothing more terrible under Heaven than the flashing eyes of a man of God. Nor more tender.

What communion did he belong to? I always thought of him as a Methodist, and indeed he was for years a Methodist minister. But now I hear that he was a Baptist, for no less a man than Dr. John Wilson immersed him as a believer at Woolwich Tabernacle. And here we are today in a Congregational church, and here it was that he loved to worship when he had a Sunday free. Such a man as he belongs to all the churches. Actually, of course, he of set purpose never joined any particular denomination. The obituary notice in the *Daily Telegraph*, reserved for the famed and renowned, tells the reason for this.

> REV. GEORGE FYFE DEMPSTER. At Westcliff-on-Sea, aged 85. Formerly known as "The Sailors' Friend". Author of religious works, he spent 42 years in dockland as welfare superintendent of The British Sailors' Society, retiring 1942. Organised International Sailors' Brotherhood.

In this Brotherhood were 22,000 members of all denominations. He kept himself free to serve them all without hindrance. He is now in the Church of the Firstborn, where these things count no longer.

You can find all your friends somewhere in the Bible. I have found him. I have him here in the Book of the Prophet Malachi. In chapter 2, verses 5 and 6, the Most High thus describes His servant, "the messenger of the Lord of Hosts":

My covenant was with him of life and peace;
And I gave them to him for the fear wherewith he reverenced Me,
for he stood in awe of My Name.

The law of truth was in his mouth,
and iniquity was not found in his lips;
he walked with Me in peace and equity,
and did turn many away from iniquity.

Now, is not that a perfect pen-portrait of our dear friend?

Think of his WORSHIP. These words are true of him: "the fear wherewith he reverenced Me. He stood in awe of My Name." As well he might, for he knew the power of that Name! He had seen it at work. His books read like an extension of The Acts of the Apostles, where they used to fling the challenge of the Name across cities and continents, finding men for Christ all the time. "In the Name of Jesus Christ of Nazareth, rise up and walk," rang out the voice of Peter across the Temple courts where shameful traders had had their earnings spilled about and found themselves whipped off the precincts by Divine fury, and across the city where He had been condemned and crucified. Whereupon a man over forty, lame from birth, felt a wondrous strength straightening his helpless limbs, got to his feet a new man in Christ, and went into church literally jumping for joy. George Dempster knew all about that. He had stood by many times and seen that miracle happen before his eyes—limping miseries of men made to leap! "His Name through faith in His Name hath made this man strong, whom ye see and know: yea, the faith which is by Him hath given him this perfect soundness in the presence of you all." And Mr. Dempster never lost the wonder of it. Half a century of such ministry never cheapened it for him, or made him take it as a matter of course. Indeed, every fresh experience of the transforming power of the Saviour's Name only made of him a more ardent worshipper. He was never far from the Holiest. He dwelt in the secret place of the Most High. He abode under the shadow of the Almighty. He never lost his awe of God.

Consider his WORDS. "The law of truth was in his mouth, and iniquity was not found in his lips." So, of course, his testimony was convincing. It was not marred by inconsistencies. For some of us, the law of truth, though faithfully preached, is spoiled by the iniquity found in our lips. George Dempster was "a white man", utterly sincere, transparently so, manifestly so, and men responded to the word of Christ which he spoke. And not only to the words spoken in a pulpit or to the perishing he was seeking to rescue. Do you know that two men doing war repairs on his house were converted?

It is, mark it well, the law of truth which the Spirit of God uses to bring men to salvation. Nothing but "the truth it as is in Jesus" will truly lead to Jesus. Our friend was always careful that what he said was God's truth, and not man's error. Let me read you a few sentences from the first book:

Promise after promise was quoted accompanied, I knew, by a power not human. "Never man spake like this Man" was true on this occasion. The purely human arguments may have had some slight effect, but it was when His Words were given that one could see how slowly but surely the victory was being won.

Observe his WALK. "He walked with Me in peace and equity." He did indeed. He walked with God. And he certainly believed in the guided life. The romance of miracle in the way he was led of the Lord, as he tells us in his books! Day by day he seems to have gone out not knowing whither he went, but assuredly knowing with Whom he was going. Not that guidance always kept him out of trouble and danger, or released him from the need of painstaking persistence and meticulous care.

Do you remember that drenching night when his congregation consisted of three people—the chapel-keeper's wife, an old lady stone deaf and her little grand-daughter? He conducted the service and preached, as though there were a crowd, himself playing the organ ("F.M.C.", 89, 90).

I went my long, wet walk homeward deeply pondering the several aspects of that evening, mostly conscious that I had anyhow discharged my duty and must leave the rest to One Who knew more about it than I did.

Only to find next time he visited that chapel that the deaf old lady had made the girl write down on her slate "all she could remember of what that gentleman had said", had been convicted of her neglect of the Saviour, had knelt down with the child and been soundly converted, and had started to pray for her three recklessly wicked sons. All three were converted, one of them the child's father.

Yes, indeed, he walked with God in peace and equity; and God found him available for His sovereign purposes. Oh, to be yielded, ready and willing like that!

And ponder his WORK. "He did turn many away from iniquity." It was his life-work. It was his only work. Hardly ever did he go out visiting or engage in the ordinary social calls of life.

He had no time: he was always on duty for his Lord: the zeal of the Lord consumed him. But can you ever estimate the worth of a life like his, morally, mentally, spiritually?

I want you to think of him in Heaven now. Not to touch upon the finer theological points of the disembodied state of our blessed dead during the waiting time until the Resurrection, we know that they are "with Christ which is far better", and that to be "absent from the body" is to be "at home with the Lord". Let that suffice for us today. Think of him there! What a welcome he must have had from his Lord! How glad all Heaven must be to have him there! And as word gets round the Glory Land, how many must be seeking him out and running to him to grip his hand! All this in terms of eternity and infinity, of course. His works do follow him. Much of his work had preceded him. Heaven is vastly richer because of his eighty-five years on earth. And, please God, his soul-saving work will still go on, though his voice is silent and his pen is still. "He being dead yet speaketh"—most likely speaking right now to conscience and heart of some soul in need here at his funeral service. Be well assured that the Saviour's arms are open to receive you now, if you do repent of your sin and self-pleasing and turn to Him as the One who died in your stead, bearing the guilt of your sin that you might be set free from it—the just for the unjust, that He might bring you to God.

For us who are the Lord's, what is the supreme challenge of G. F. Dempster's life? Has he one secret above all others? I am sure of it. All is summed up in one word: LOVE. See how he brought it into his subsequent titles. "Touched by a Loving Hand." "The Love that Will Not Let Me Go." "Lovest Thou Me?" Love never faileth. Love is the answer. Love is His way. "Why," asked a dear friend of mine only last Sunday, "why are not more of us so filled with the Holy Ghost as he was?" I can only suppose it is because we are not prepared for the cost of the most costly factor in this world—love—that cost God Calvary. Yet, to be sure, we have it. "The love of God is shed abroad in our hearts by the Holy Spirit Who is given unto us." It is there: it but needs to be developed and cultivated—at a price. O God, raise up more of his like, for such a time as this! And begin here with those of us who loved him and owe so much to him!

But who am I to be saying these things to you? Let the great man himself have the last word at his own funeral service. I beg leave to read yet once again; and I am reading from the closing pages of "Finding Men for Christ".

> It must have been some such scene as we now witness in the City streets which caused our Lord's sorrow when His prophetic vision " beheld the City and wept over it". Yet we who call ourselves by His Name and profess to love Him feel little or no anguish or even concern as we see the crowds of lost sheep. Is it "because iniquity abounds" that "the love of many" has "grown cold"? That is how He put it as He looked across the space of time and saw our day. . . .
>
> If our petty selfishness could but be overcome; if sectarian dissensions, if doctrinal prejudices, if pride and arrogance and unbrotherliness could be exchanged for a rebaptism of His Spirit, there are enough disciples in this grand old country of ours alone to win the world for Him and to find all the lost men now living in conditions unspeakable. . . .
>
> We are responsible. The Church is responsible—and by "the Church" I mean every single individual member of it in all its various sections. This is an urgent plea that all who call themselves Christians should cease to spend precious hours in fruitless contention about non-essentials, and more earnestly seek, either by concerted action or individual effort, to find lost souls and bring them to Christ.

THE QUIET MOMENT

I know
That He who lives above the Stars
Dwells also here with every humble soul;
That He who made us what we are
And fashioned all the Universe,
Speaks yet to make the broken-hearted whole.

I know
I cannot go beyond His reach,
Nor roam so far my track He cannot see;
Toss'd on wild seas, or stranded on the beach.
He will not leave me quite alone,
But e'en "unto the end" is still with me.

I know
That as I gaze above to azure height,
Or peer below the waters deep to sound,
Or revel in the fragrance and the sight
Of all the new-born Nature's offspring sweet,
He's there—and ever must in all be found.

He knows
That I, in all my blundering steps,
Would fain direct my way to Heaven above,
That, failing in my striving to be good,
I'm grieved that He should find me so,
And long to know that He forgives in love.

G. F. D.

THE LIFE HE LIVED

’Tis easy to laugh when the world laughs too,
  But hard to be strong
    When the days go wrong;
’Tis easy enough to sing when the trouble is through,
  But I want the might
    To stick to the right
When everyone takes just the opposite view.

G. F. D.

THE LIFE HE LIVED

GEORGE FYFE DEMPSTER was born at Plumstead in March 1871. His father was a talented graduate of Aberdeen University, his mother coming from the Isle of Sheppey on the Kent coast. George knew in his own home the danger of strong drink, which must have formed in him such strong total abstinence principles and engendered in him later on a passion for rescuing men from its thraldom.

He was a really naughty boy, as most great men seem to have been! There came a time, however, when he determined to be good. One Sunday evening, in the gallery of the Plumstead Common Methodist Church, all went well—almost ominously for such as he. The good resolutions failed when, feeling in his trousers pocket for a handkerchief, he discovered that some of his marbles were there. Down the gallery steps they were rolled, tumbling noisily one by one. An old steward leaping to his side said, "Really, Dempster, this is too much. Out you go!" Out he went, with more force than he had come in. Never did he go into that chapel again until years later, as a local preacher, he started to mount the pulpit stairs and the same old steward was in the front pew and recognised him. "Praise the Lord, Dempster!" he said, in a voice that rang through the building.

We have no details of his conversion: his own record simply says that he gave himself to the Lord in 1887. It may well be that, having been ejected from the chapel on the hill, he found his way, with thousands of others, to the great Baptist Tabernacle in Woolwich. We do know that the year after his conversion, at the age of seventeen, he was immersed as a believer by Dr. John Wilson, for whom he cherished a life-long regard. At the age of nineteen, seeking to serve the Saviour Whom he had come to trust and love and feeling the urge of the prophet within his soul, he became a Methodist local preacher, three years later taking charge of a derelict mission church housed in a tin chapel in Plumstead. The great Head of the Church in

Heaven immediately set His seal upon this work and there was a steady stream of conversions. Here began his life's work of seeking and "finding men for Christ". He gathered about him a band of keen young people and organised cycle teams of witness in all directions. He himself was an ardent cyclist and began on a "penny-farthing". He always had a very powerful voice in the open air, and he used to practise voice production in a ravine on Plumstead Common.

During this time he earned his living as a servant of the War Office in Woolwich Arsenal. His passionate preaching of peace and the stand he took against going to war aroused no little hostility amongst the men in the Arsenal. It was one day in 1900 when he was praying in his office with one of his colleagues, as his daily custom was, that there suddenly intruded into their prayers a surge of angry voices. He realised that it was most likely he they were after, but decided with his friend to keep on their knees and not let this disturbance interrupt their prayer-time. The voices died away and silence ensued, which seemed remarkable. Actually it was the news of the relief of Mafeking which had just come through and had diverted the angry mob. His tenure as a Civil Servant was to be short-lived, and it was actually the Boer War that flung him out of the War Office. He was a highly skilled worker and had risen rapidly to a position of authority, but became convinced that he could no longer continue authorising the making of guns and helping in their manufacture. It was he, by the way, who had to give the statistics of ammunitions for Africa to Mr. Joseph Chamberlain. Throwing up this good job, therefore, for conscience sake, he offered his service as a minister in the East End Methodist Mission and was appointed to the pastoral care of "The Old Mahogany Bar" in Whitechapel. Interestingly enough, a year later he was called back to the Arsenal, and the men who had booed him and at one time had been lusting after his blood presented him with a Bible, the head of the Arsenal presiding. They must have realised that he was sincere—a man of peace deep down in his heart and not only by word of mouth. Some pacifists seem to put the emphasis on the third syllable. But not he—nor on the second. To the last, he could never bear resentments. "Oh, forget it!" he would say.

As many young men do, he worked far too hard and had to be confined to bed. He heard the doctor say outside his bedroom door that there was no hope, realised that his work could not possibly be finished and, with a cry in his heart to the Lord, determined to get better, and from that hour turned the corner. As a matter of fact, he continually wore himself out, and rarely took a day off. It is manifestly true that hard work never kills anyone, though there is a heavy death-rate annually from lack of it. He lived to the age of eighty-four and had sentence of death on himself for the last seventeen years. A Harley Street specialist said that he would never work again, but he was wrong, and Mr. Dempster was in harness to the end. Truly a fitting epitaph for this hard worker would be in his Master's words: "He that loseth his life shall find it."

It was while he was still at Woolwich Arsenal that he took unto himself a wife. On July 4th, 1896, at Plumstead Common Methodist Church, the boy with the pocket full of marbles, now an esteemed member of the preaching fraternity, was married to Miss Martha Miller, one of a large family worshipping in that church. With her husband she was called upon to leave a suburban villa on the Thames-side hills of Plumstead for a home above "The Old Mahogany Bar", in Grace's Alley, Cable Street. This little corner of the East End has survived all the bombing. Mrs. Dempster died in 1937, leaving one daughter who lived with her father to the end: indeed, she was never separated from him, not even for holidays.

A few years later he was put in charge of the Lycett Mission in Mile End Road, Stepney. At that time he was associated with Toynbee Hall in many branches of social service. He was elected as its representative on the Mile End Board of Guardians, became Chairman of the Hospital Committee and a member of other medical councils—the Mental After-Care Committee, etc., etc. We have some of his speeches delivered during those years, terrible with the passion of the reformer and tender with the compassion of the pastor. He began personal investigations into labour conditions in the docks, housing of the poor, etc., and wrote a series of articles entitled "The Extra Casual", giving his experiences as an amateur docker, under the *nom de plume* of

Geoffrey Dee. Some of these were quoted in the House of Commons. Through these years, too, he was actively engaged with Archbishop Cosmo Gordon Lang, when he was Bishop of Stepney, the great Methodist leader Dr. J. Alfred Sharp, and others, in promoting the Children's Bill and the Licensing Bill of 1908.

In connection with the last named, a week of meetings was held at the East End Mission. Bishop Lang, Dr. Sharp and G. F. Dempster could have been seen processing together around the main roads of East London as a public protest. Gangs of men were paid to disturb and break up both meetings and processions. On the Friday evening of that week there was complete respite from interruption. Dr. Sharp said, "Our prayers have been heard and there is silence tonight," to which Mr. Dempster said, "I don't like the sound of this silence, Sharp: I think it's ominous." After the meeting, having taken Dr. Sharp to Stepney Station, he walked home with two B.B. boys to his house in Carlton Square. Taken by surprise in ambush, he was attacked. He laid about him, and to escape from the ruffians, fell into an open shop doorway where a Jewish greengrocer was polishing a brass scoop for his scales. One of the gang picked up this scoop, cut the eye out of the greengrocer and rushing at George Dempster wrenched out thirteen teeth at one blow. Ever after this he suffered denture discomfort, not even the most skilful dentist being able perfectly to fit him. Meanwhile the two boys had run to fetch the police. One of them, interestingly enough, was the younger brother of the far-famed Bombardier Wells. Having taken Mr. Dempster home, the police forbade him to appear next day. "I must be there tomorrow night at all costs," he said; and seeing that he was quite determined, the police gave him protection and were there about him all the time.

It would be in place here to mention some of his other friends. Harold Begbie and he were naturally kindred spirits. Arthur Mee used to call him "St. George", to which George Dempster reprisalled with "Prince Arthur". It was Hugh Redwood who encouraged him to write and gave him the necessary thrust to begin his great literary work. He was also very friendly with Sir William (later Lord) Beveridge, and for many years maintained a close comradeship with Mr. Robert Carnegie and his family. All children were his friends. None was shy or awkward with him, for he had the genius of love to make them happy, either in twos or threes or in little groups. He used to tell with a chuckle of one very cold morning in the Lycett ministry. He had been called early to a sick man, and on the way home to breakfast was accosted by a small waif of a girl. "Mister, does yer fink in your own mind I shall come to the Kissmas Tree?" It was only for those who had made so many attendances during the year, but this mite was looked after in other ways. Inasmuch!

In 1911 he was called back to Plumstead to undertake a building scheme and to extend the work begun in 1893. The new church was opened and filled in 1914. Two years later, while the First World War was at its height, the Head of the Church transferred him to another part of the ministry, which was to become his real life work. He was called to take charge of the missionary and welfare work of the British and Foreign Sailors' Society, as it was then called. This he continued until 1942, when the age limit imposed retirement upon him, but he still retained the Secretaryship of the International Sailors' Brotherhood which he had inaugurated in May 1917.

Though for so many years he had been giving himself in the service of men, it was not until 1935 that those books of his which have made his name world-famous were published. "Finding Men for Christ" was the first, and immediately became a best seller, being translated into many languages and still in great demand in many parts of the world, as are "The Love that Will not Let Me Go", 1937; "Touched by a Loving Hand", 1939; and "Lovest Thou Me?", 1944.

On September 1st, 1938, at the Union Church, Woodford, he ended his sorrowful loneliness by marrying an East London lady—for twenty years a worker among the Methodists of Barking and caring for a widowed mother—whose business acumen and efficiency had matched his own, one who by dint of mathematical ability and agility, as well as by persuasive wisdom, had attained to a responsible position of trust in business.

His time of retirement, as is so often the case, became even busier than ever. He travelled widely, preaching and lecturing in churches of all denominations throughout the British Isles; and as his books became more and more widely known, appeals for aid in tragic cases of broken lives reached him by almost every mail. He was never one to spare himself, and the pursuit of these lost ones involved him in much wearing travel and intimate correspondence, as well as marvellous proofs of what he used to describe as "God's appointments". Incidentally, at his express wish, every one of these personal letters has been carefully destroyed and any photographs returned to relatives. Every Thursday he went to Limehouse for the day on his Brotherhood work connected with the British Sailors' Society. He never sought for himself either position or fame or comfort, always giving himself out for others. That, of course, is the secret of blessing and also of inner renewal and all providence. Christian Unions in hundreds wanted him in these later years and really out-wore his strength. He helped to inaugurate a Christian Union for Probation Officers.

Under the gentle and ingenious care of his wife, he was maintained in health almost to the end. He rejoiced in the work of Dr. Billy Graham and in all that transpired, and enjoyed a preview of the film "Souls in Conflict" at the Stoll Theatre, a few evenings later taking his wife, on her birthday, to Westminster Central Hall for the Annual Carol Service by the London Emmanuel Choir. The next day, in spite of its being December and his being far from well, he went out into the garden to put back a fence which had blown over; but he should not have been there, and it was that that made him take to his bed. On Christmas Day they thought he had gone. In March the doctor's verdict one day was that he could not possibly live the night. But he rallied. His eighty-fourth birthday was a day of peculiar joy. He was so much better that morning that he said to his dear wife, "I am going to enjoy my birthday." He certainly did. In his room were flowers of almost every variety procurable in March; a home-made birthday cake; several visitors; feeling stronger in himself—such a happy day! The untiring nursing went on until the summer days of May gave him enough strength sometimes to go downstairs. After Whitsun a friend drove him by car to Westcliff, where he used to sit in the sun each day, but all the time losing ground. Hotel life is not ideal for a sick man. The day before he died he took a bus ride to the shops to buy a brooch for his wife. But his strength was gone; and on the next evening he was not, for God took him. At his funeral service many ministers, leaders and workers were present—a gathering widely representative of Christian enterprises. In keeping with the Greatheart we mourned, there were no flowers, by request. Any gifts were to be sent to one of his interests and cares, the Mission of Hope, Croydon.

This is a scrappy survey of a long and eventful life, but almost every page of his books reveals the man and his work. They were never written for this purpose, of course, for he was the last man in this world to parade himself; but none the less in telling of the grace of God in the men he found for Christ, the human partner of the Divine seeker is portrayed. There are also gruesome adventures and hair-breadth escapes which cannot yet be told because they happened in the service of his country in times of desperate international emergency. Suffice it to say that it is only through the providence of God that he died in his bed.

Whenever he pronounced the benediction in public or in private he almost invariably referred to "the Morning". He lived with his thoughts towards the sun rising. And until the eternal dawn broke for him he had been used of God to bring many a soul to the new morning of salvation.

G. R. K.

KEEP true to the Highest,
  Keep faith with thy Lord;
He ever is nighest,
  And sweet is His Word,
There's no day too trying
  For Him to control,
No soul near to dying
  But He can console.
In Life's thickest battle
  He's there on Thy side;
In times of grave peril
  He safely will guide.

G. F. D.

God is here, need I worry?
  He full well knows every care;
Time is His, need I hurry?
  He doth every burden share.

G. F. D.

It matters not who whispers blame
  If God sees I am right;
The world knows not my secret aim,
  Nor understands my fight.

G. F. D.

THE WORK HE DID

UNTIL HE FIND IT

(Luke xv, 4)

"*For the Son of Man is come to seek and to save that which was lost.*" (Luke xix, 10.)

Further records of His "seekings" and "findings"
in which He graciously permits
human co-operation

"*Likewise, I say unto you, there is joy in the presence of the angels of God over one sinner that repenteth.*" (Jesus, as recorded in Luke xv, 10.)

FOREWORD

THE author has received much encouragement from evidences which have reached him from many parts of the world that readers have been blest by the reading of earlier records. He prays that these further instances of God's unceasing love may influence some to yield their lives to the Lord Jesus Christ, and thus know Him to be "The Way, the Truth, and the Life".

Snaresbrook,
*London, E.*18.

GEO. F. DEMPSTER

"*And when he came to himself, he said, I will arise and go to my Father.*" (Luke xv, 17-18.)

One

"Then drew near to Him all the publicans and sinners for to hear Him." (Luke xv, 1.)

IN the Gospels this fact is recorded again and again, and it was to such that He had a special attraction.

So it is still today. He is the only hope for a world so obviously full of lost souls; a distracted world trying all manner of expedients unavailingly, yet neglecting the one way to peace.

The only way to peace among men is peace with God Who is being so widely ignored.

When the "dearly loved physician", as Luke is described by the Apostle Paul in his letter to the Colossians (Col. iv, 14), recorded the words which form the title of this book, he was doubtless very deeply impressed that such a phrase should have fallen from the Saviour's lips, expressing so unmistakably the inexhaustible patience of the Seeker of men's souls.

However far away the wanderer should roam, His love would not let him go. The search would continue.

So through the long ages until this very day He has sought and is still seeking the souls of men and of nations.

Alas! that our human response is so unwilling. Lost souls are all about us, not only among those whose folly and sin has led them into disgrace, degradation and poverty, but also in homes where outwardly there are few visible signs of the tragic spiritual conditions prevailing.

It is true also to assert that in our congregations in places of worship, maybe quite unknown to the preacher, are lost souls whom the Lord is seeking and hoping to find through His messenger by the Holy Spirit. Disappointed in their unguided searching for satisfaction, and for the solution of their personal, domestic or even business problems, they attend God's house, listen to His Word, and even join in uttering prayers and words of praise, yet are lost because Christ has not yet become their acknowledged Guide and Saviour.

One October day my morning mail brought me a letter from a dear Christian lady who had been reading "Finding Men for Christ", and, as she put it, felt it had come into her hands as a messenger.

"Can you help us to find R . . . for whom we have been seeking and praying?" Some details and a photograph were enclosed. His present location was unknown to his family and friends, but he had been in disgrace in London, and certain clues had been followed up with painful results, revealing how sadly the prodigal had fallen by stages into disgrace and despair. If only he could be found and brought to realise his need of Christ's pardon and power, how grateful his friend would be. He had been in serious trouble through drunkenness and law-breaking, but had for a long time failed to respond to attempts to locate him.

Prayer was being continued that, as in certain instances recorded in that book, the author might be used of God to find R . . .

So, another quest was added to the already long list of similar seekings. Doss-houses, hospitals, police stations, night clubs and other haunts of such deluded individuals were investigated, but three months passed without any apparent success.

Then, one Sunday morning just as one was preparing to leave home for a distant preaching appointment, the telephone bell rang.

After confirming the number, the caller announced, "This is Police Sergeant —— who, knowing that you are trying to trace a young man named R . . ., is unofficially able to tell you that one bearing that name is due to surrender to his bail at —— Court tomorrow morning at ten o'clock, and I thought he might be your man."

"Thank you very much, Sergeant. God willing, I'll be there."

That Monday morning in early January was bitterly cold and forbidding, but, realising that prayer was being answered, the journey was made and watch was kept near the Court as the crowds of men and women hurried past to their places of employment. Every tall man was scrutinised until one appeared in striking contrast to the warmly clad ones. He had no overcoat or wrap but a tightly buttoned thin jacket, and was obviously without warm underclothing. His features wan and sad, his gait lingering. Yes, he bore resemblance to the portrait in my pocket.

"Excuse me, is your name Mr. R . . .?" I asked him.

Rather startled he replied, "Yes, sir; that is my name."

"And you are going into that police station?"

"Yes, sir!"

"Then I'm coming in with you."

There was no further word spoken as we crossed the road together and ascended the few steps into the open doorway. There a smiling police sergeant accosted us.

"You know this young man, Mr. Dempster?"

"No, Sergeant, I do not. I've only just met him for the first time. Nor do I know you."

Then I learned once again how the Lord plans His seeking "until He find".

"I was at the Annual Meeting of the International Christian Police Association recently, sir, when you addressed us. I also learned that you had been inquiring for a man of this name—so unofficially I 'phoned you yesterday, and am glad to be of use. But you would like to speak for the accused?"

"I certainly would, if possible."

"That is being arranged, sir."

Then R . . . was directed to the office and I was taken into the crowded court, where there were assembled solicitors, policemen, witnesses and the usual motley crowd of people who for one reason or another gather, especially on Monday mornings, at police courts. A sad comment upon public taste. But this morning there was something of a diversion.

There was already standing in the prisoners' dock a bedraggled, miserable specimen of humanity who was wildly gesticulating and shouting in the broadest Irish, which I could scarcely understand, in an endeavour to convince the magistrate that it was not he who had assaulted that sixteen-stone constable, but the reverse.

The whole assembly was laughing at his persistent effort despite the attempted intervention of the constables who sought to restrain him. Even the Bench could scarcely keep countenance, but at length his Worship obtained a hearing and advised the prisoner to "take a month's holiday to think things over".

The next prisoner was brought in—R . . . stood at attention and evidently impressed those present as one of a different type. There was perfect silence while at once there stepped into the witness-box the sergeant who had met us at the door.

"Your Worship," he began, causing the legal people and the police of various ranks to stare at the unusual interruption of the court procedure.

The magistrate, holding his spectacles in his hand, looked questioningly at the speaker for a moment, indicating interest.

"Before the next prisoner is tried there is a gentleman in court who would like to speak to you concerning him," said the sergeant.

"Oh! oh! Who is he?" questioned the magistrate—rather testily, I thought.

The name was mentioned, and to my astonishment instead of a rebuke to the sergeant, the magistrate said quite eagerly:

"I'll hear him."

Again I felt distinctly that my Lord was guiding, but I did not then know that sitting in his place of authority was another whose heart was aching for news of a missing one, nor that he too had been reading the records of the great Seeker of souls in that same little book. The name given arrested his attention.

"What would you like to say, sir?" he said to me as I was invited to the witness-box.

What a challenge! What an opportunity! What would I like to say? I had not been told to hold the copy of the Scriptures provided for witnesses while they declared they would "speak the truth, the whole truth and nothing but the truth".

But "What would I like to say?"

In my heart was the prayer, "Lord, what wouldst Thou have me to do?"

Thanking the magistrate for his permission, while everyone listened, and knowing that brevity was essential, I began.

"I would like to say, sir, with your permission, that although the accused may have broken the law and is liable to be convicted, he is not a criminal. He is a prodigal. And you know, sir, that in this little book I now hold in my hand there is a story of a prodigal. You know, sir, what a prodigal is? I am here on behalf of Him Who told that incomparable story to say that, if by the clemency of this Court, this young man could be set at liberty, I would undertake to ensure his return to his broken-hearted family across the sea."

The magistrate was obviously moved, although no word was spoken to me. Instead, leaning down toward the Clerk of the Court, he conversed with the latter for several minutes, while in perfect silence the whole of those present listened.

The charge was read to the prisoner, in answer to which he pleaded "Guilty".

"Yes!" said his Worship. "We know you are guilty. You have done this thing before. You were warned on the last occasion you were here that if you came before us again charged with stealing books at one shop and offering them for sale at another, you would be punished, and now I must fulfil that warning. You should be sent to prison. But did you hear what that gentleman said just now from the witness-box? Did you? Did you hear every word of it?"

"Yes, sir," answered R . . . "I did."

There was a moment's quiet pause, as if the magistrate was considering how best he could explain his intention. Meanwhile I was observing the police inspectors and other officials and also the legal gentlemen present. All eyes were intently turned toward the Bench.

"But I have a mind to do an unusual thing this morning," said the magistrate. "The prisoner has broken the law, has pleaded guilty and must be punished."

Then, addressing R . . . by name, he asked him: "If, by the clemency of this Court, you could be set at liberty, would you go with that gentleman, do as he asks you, and promise never to repeat your offences? Would you?"

To me it seemed almost a pleading, and later I felt confirmed in this.

"Yes, sir!" answered R . . . promptly.

Another brief pause, during which his Worship conferred again with the Clerk sitting beneath him.

Resuming his upright position the magistrate voiced his decision, still, I felt, with the same persuasive tone.

"R . . ., instead of sending you to prison, a heavy fine will be inflicted. Upon payment of that fine of —— you will be discharged; and I hope you will keep your promise just made to this Court."

R . . . uttered a quiet "Thank you, sir!" and was conducted by a policeman from the Court. I followed, being prepared to meet the fine.

As we proceeded along the corridor we passed a burly policeman sitting at a desk. I heard him mutter to R . . . as he preceded me, "You're a lucky dog. You've got a pal somewhere."

Such an opportunity could not be missed. Holding up my pocket Testament, I rejoined:

"Yes, officer, he has! He has the finest Friend any man ever had or ever will have; and His Name is in this book. Do you know it? His Friend's Name is Jesus."

The policeman hung his head.

The fine was paid, and R . . . and I had left the premises, crossing the road at the spot where we had first met. R . . . was asking me how it came about that I was there. He had heard of me, but never expected to meet me.

"Ah! but you have other friends who love you and have been praying for you. Their prayers are now being answered," I explained.

At that point we were interrupted by a young policeman who had followed us, and touching me upon my shoulder said:

"Excuse me, sir, but could you spare time to return to the station? One of my colleagues would like to speak with you."

"Certainly," I answered, rather wonderingly.

I was led back into the police station, where there awaited one holding open the door of a room marked "Private". He closed the door as I entered, and facing me was the man who had spoken to R . . . as we passed him in the corridor.

"Sir," he began, "I heard all that transpired in the Court this morning, and I hope you have forgiven my rudeness. But I also ask your help. My dear wife and I have an only daughter who is breaking our hearts by her conduct. We do not know where she is. Could you help us to find our girl?"

Thus, within an hour, two further searches for "lost" ones were requested.

Returning to R . . ., it was a thrill to hear him say eagerly, "Mr. Dempster, I am that prodigal of whom you spoke, and I need that Saviour."

"Splendid! Now we must tell Him so. Where do you lodge when you have the means to pay?"

"I'll take you, sir."

He led me through the crowded thoroughfares to a place where, in a room at the back of the premises, there were a number of small iron bedstead frames covered with filthy bedding, beside one of which we knelt as he poured out his contrite prayer for pardon and power.

"You sleep here in this unhealthy state, when you could dwell so happily in your own home with your dear ones. Why?"

"Because I am that prodigal, and now I realise it. So, by the help of God, I am returning to Him and to them," he said, amid his tears.

By a series of further remarkable interventions of the Holy Spirit we were enabled to get him to his distant home, and I am able to record not only that he was indeed made a "new creature", but that he has become a "fisher of men" in truly wonderful ways, praising his Lord that, "while he was yet a great way off", he was found.

A volume could be written concerning the enabling of this disciple to reach the many who today praise God for R . . .'s patient witnessing and pleading, which has meant immeasurable blessing to scores of others, who, like himself, have discovered that our Saviour pursues the search "until He finds" the lost one.

But, as of old, the Christ needs those to whom He can say as He did that evening long ago, "the night before He was betrayed",

"Ye have not chosen me, but I have chosen you and ordained you, that ye should go and bring forth fruit, and that your fruit should remain." (John xv, 16.)

He calls us to become, each in some special way that only He could devise and plan, "fishers of men".

This is His commission still to the Church on earth. But we are too busy, too encumbered, too distracted often, to even hear His Voice as He calls us to some urgent bit of service, the patient carrying out of which would astonish us by its "fruit".

An instance of this follows in the next story.

Two

"My ways are higher than your ways."
"For my thoughts are not your thoughts, neither are your ways my ways, saith the Lord." (Isa. lv, 8.)

"WHEN are you giving us another book?" is a question asked in letters reaching me from many parts of the world and by people I meet in various parts of this country following evangelical services.

The previous records have found their way into far-distant lands, into ships at sea and into most remote regions. They are printed in many languages, with the result that, falling into the hands of someone who, suffering anxiety over some relative or friend who has strayed and become "lost", is immediately awakened to the possibility that the lost one might be found if only an earnest and God-directed search were made by someone sufficiently interested and willing to seek for clues and follow them up.

In other words, the case having apparently become one in which the ordinary treatment has not proved efficacious, there is need to call in a specialist who can examine the symptoms, diagnose the malady and prescribe the right treatment with hope of a cure.

The cure of physical ills often necessitates deep research, very considerable skill, constant vigilance and attention, with the addition of the discoveries of science, and an understanding of the conditions which cause the trouble.

Human bodies vary considerably even when only the material organism is being treated. Indeed, there are no two bodies exactly alike, and remedies applied successfully in one case may not be so effective in another. Doctors differ in their diagnoses and prognoses, therefore also in their treatment. The human body is most wonderfully constructed, but there are certain unalterable conditions governing physical sickness. It can be located as an affliction affecting a definite part of the structure: the foot, the eye, the internal organs, the spine, the heart and so on. In such instances the practitioner makes his decision as to a course of action to be followed and prescribes accordingly.

But soul sickness is a vastly different thing. It baffles all the known methods of research. Its symptoms are often so incalculable as to deceive even the patient himself. No human is wise enough to comprehend its real character. Its varied forms are so many that no pharmacology could describe it. Its danger is immeasurable, and, unless treated by the only Physician capable of dealing with it, is inevitably fatal.

The Church of Jesus Christ has been informed, instructed and trained to use the infallible remedy, but alas, is only very casually applying it. Supposed palliatives are preferred while all the time souls are dying all around.

Yet there is abounding evidence that wherever the true Specific is applied with patience and diligence sin-sick souls can be revived and given new life.

"The Gospel of Christ is the power of God *unto salvation* to every one that believeth" (Romans i, 16).

That truth has to be accepted, believed and applied in every case of soul-sickness, of whatever nature or kind, and these records are evidence of its effectiveness. The tragedy is that while many agree that it is so, they are apathetic in dealing with the malady itself. When our Saviour faced that hostile crowd of "publicans and sinners" (Luke xv) He was aware that some of those who listened to Him would recognise the special significance of the illustrations He was using to teach them God's character and love.

Probably there was such a "prodigal" among the "sinners", or maybe such a father as the "certain man" of whom He spoke. Possibly also an "elder brother".

If that be so, the effect upon those whom the "cap fitted" can be imagined.

The records printed in these books have similarly reached many readers and many homes where sorrow has followed the going "into a far country" of some loved one. The result has been a pathetic letter to the author beseeching his friendly prayerful aid to "find" the missing one. Scores of such appeals have been acknowledged sympathetically; and wherever possible some action has been taken. In some instances there have been results, which could never have been imagined by any of those concerned. In others it would seem that the one being sought had so covered up his or her tracks that each human attempt had been futile—or, the fugitive so constantly evaded the seeker that the longed-for result had not been so far possible.

In many cases there is no evidence of penitence or desire for amendment. Like the evil spirits of whom Jesus spoke, they cry, "Let us alone! Let us alone! What have we to do with thee, Jesus of Nazareth?"

But such conditions do not deter the Divine Shepherd Who "seeketh until He findeth"—and Who patiently, persistently guides those who co-operate with Him in the search.

He has manifold ministries, and often astonishes us by the means He employs to lead the straying one back to the fold.

On the other hand, the devices of evil are subtle and intricate. Not always "as a roaring lion" does the Devil go about seeking whom he may destroy. Plausible and cunning are the allurements which attract and entice the victims of sin. In many guises and shapes the Tempter approaches the unwatchful and the weak.

It is incredible that in "Christian" England we still permit, and even legalise, those agencies which everyone is aware are designed for the express purpose of trapping and betraying the unwary and the foolish. We profess to be concerned about the moral degeneration of our age, yet condone and foster the causes thereof.

Every social and religious worker knows that whatever theories we might hold as to heredity, it is through eye-gate and ear-gate that the enemy most easily gains access to the souls of people—especially the young. Yet newspapers, hoardings, picture-houses, wireless sets often purvey poisonous ideas by suggestive word or picture which sow seeds of a fearful harvest for days to come. There is but one antidote—the love of God shed abroad in the hearts of men, women and children.

So, while pursuing the search for those who have been led astray, we urge all who have the privilege to spread the knowledge of Him Who alone can enlighten and strengthen the young wills in order to prevent such straying.

Many of those with whom we have had to do have not been altogether without a knowledge of Christ, but have very deliberately chosen to follow the attractions of the world, the flesh and the Devil. Having made this choice, it has soon been proven to them that "the way of transgressors is hard", there being neither satisfaction nor peace of mind. Even the first fair promises soon failed them, and as time passed, self-control weakened and they became aware of their subservience to habits they could not break. Such is the oft-repeated story. Many have said to the present writer when urged to forsake evil ways: "I cannot now break with it," and some have even expressed the still worse attitude: "I don't want to change. Why should I?"

Many there are, however, who, for lack of a friendly human influence, continue drifting, drifting, away from safety and happiness, and becoming more and more difficult to recover.

The records hitherto published have not only brought large numbers of fresh requests for help; they have inspired many Christians to attempt service of similar kinds, with results which have brought joy to many hearts.

Here a word of gentle warning is needful. There is but one example, but one Person Whom it is safe to emulate.

The Word of God is a safe guide; and He Who said "I am the Way" is the only Pattern for our service in the great work of winning men for the Kingdom of God.

Just as in the physical field many nostrums are speciously advertised to be "the cure for body ills", so many "false doctrines" are said to be the way to mental and spiritual healing. False teachers have arisen who cry "This way", as is foretold in the Scriptures, and who lead many astray by belittling and even denying the teaching of the Bible.

There is, for instance, the rising tide of Communism, which, by promising those who ignorantly accept and follow its false and cruel leaders a better world, seduces them and lures them into accepting a way of life which is wholly materialistic and tyrannical, entirely devoid of the Christian virtues and qualities.

But there is also another rising tide. A great heart-hunger is one of the causes of a widespread inquiry, especially among the younger people of many nations, concerning the Christian faith and its eternal values.

The faithful proclamation of the Gospel of Jesus Christ by spoken word and loyal living is bearing fruit among the new literates as well as among those whose privilege it is to inherit the results of godliness in parentage and association.

At a certain hospital just off one of London's busiest thoroughfares, for the control of which, as the Chairman of its Management Committee, I was largely responsible, having completed one of my regular tours of inspection with the Medical Officer-in-Charge and other officials, we adjourned to the M.O.'s sitting-room for our usual cup of tea and more or less confidential chat.

He and I were on completely happy terms, and in most matters quite in harmony as to procedure. The many subjects of serious concern relating to the buildings, the wards, the staff, the dietary and so on called for a great deal of discussion before being brought before the regular meetings of the full Committee for final decisions and adoption.

Hence we were often necessarily brought together, and found a good deal of mutual interest.

But there was one subject upon which we had some divergence of view.

Whenever one mentioned the matter of personal religion there was an immediate and quite obvious attempt to "change the subject".

Observing this in quite the early stages of our acquaintance, I was, of course, careful to guard against giving offence, while always feeling that in some suitable way the difficulty should be overcome.

Many occasions were used to properly lead up to the vital question of his own condition of heart, but always he avoided the issue by turning the topic of conversation, usually into a matter of serious importance to the work of the hospital of which he was becoming proud.

So it was difficult on these occasions when obviously he purposely blocked the way to pursue the desire one had to know where he stood.

Then one day the great opportunity occurred.

A member of the staff, in whom I had shown some interest, passed us just as we had concluded our rounds and were adjourning to Doctor's sitting-room.

He had observed this man's acknowledgment of my friendly "Good afternoon, Mr. S . . .!" as we passed, and commented upon it.

"You know Mr S . . ., do you not?"

"Yes, I've known him quite a long time."

"He is very interesting and quite good at his work," he continued. "I like him and will keep an eye upon him."

"Has he told you anything of his story?" I asked.

"No! Has he a story?"

Here was my long-awaited opportunity. I would seize it.

"Oh yes! He has a story: a rather wonderful story. Would you care to hear it? I believe it would interest you and would not be regarded as a breach of confidence if it were told you."

We were now sitting awaiting the arrival of the refreshments which were always forthcoming when the Chairman and doctor were known to have finished their peregrination.

"Yes, please tell me, if you so wish."

"Well, it will take a little while to relate, but I've the feeling that when you hear it you will be not only interested but possibly greatly surprised—and perhaps helped."

He seemed a bit startled by that remark, but did not question its significance.

"It is about seven years since I first met S . . ., and it came about in a singular way. You are aware that in my vocation there is a great diversity of procedure. It is not alone in the pulpit that one seeks to gain an entrance into the hearts of one's hearers; but for some of us there are special, and oft-times peculiar ways of doing so."

Here he interrupted with, I thought, an eagerness which was a new feature.

"Yes, I've heard something of your own strange methods of getting hold of men and women. But do go on with this story."

I was only too ready to do so, for the best of reasons.

"Yes! About seven years ago I was one day visiting a business house in the West End, the owner of which had often helped me by employing men who were on my hands and in whom I was interested for their spiritual good.

"I was searching for a prodigal whom I had traced to this office, where men spent their time addressing envelopes at so much per thousand for advertising purposes. The business was run as a commercial concern, but those who controlled it were also philanthropists, for, in addition to the money they paid the writers for addressing the circulars, wrappers and envelopes, they provided beds and meals upon the premises at remarkably cheap rates, thus offering real help to men whose circumstances are such that aid of this kind was urgently needed.

"For certain reasons handwritten addresses were preferred to typewritten, printed or duplicated, by those who engaged this firm to do their work; and naturally men whose handwriting was clear and distinct were selected. This again implied that among the men chosen were many who had once held better positions. Among them I knew of those who had been civil servants, cashiers, bank clerks, accountants, as well as some who held collegiate degrees. One had held the office of Lord Mayor of his city. Several had been clergymen. Here they were, sitting at long tables, with piles of folded papers or envelopes, working side by side, scarcely knowing who their neighbour was, scribbling away at as swift a pace as possible in order to earn a few shillings—some much more adept than others."

All this I explained to my doctor friend who had never previously heard of such a place. Then I continued:

"I inquired of the head of this concern how my own protégés were progressing; who had left; who still remained, and so on; and then described the man for whom I was searching."

"'Yes! He has been here for a couple of weeks, but has vanished, as so many do, leaving no trace. But there is a man here who was very friendly with him. We'll ask if he can give us a clue.'

"The acquaintance was questioned, but beyond the fact that my man had left one morning without repaying a small amount he had borrowed, he could not help me at all.

"I had left the building and was walking along Ludgate Hill

observing the men who in those days were allowed to stand in the gutter hawking various articles for sale to passers-by, when I suddenly came upon a tall, well-built man, clad in a suit of white material trimmed with scarlet facings, buttons, etc. offering paper bags containing 'Maizey-Pop' for sale. It was the man for whom I had been searching. We had met only once before during my search for him, but our recognition now was mutual. Endeavouring to avoid my recognising him, he had, upon seeing me approaching, turned to walk hurriedly away. That I could not allow. I soon overtook and confronted him.

"'What does this mean, S . . .? Have you come to this?'

"'Yes!' he replied. 'I have let you down again. I've been drinking and gambling; and, Padre, there is no hope for me. I simply can't resist it. Don't bother any more about me.'

"Then, as if compelling himself to do an unavoidable thing, he burst out:

"'Do you know how my wife and boy are?'

"'Yes! I know how they are. They were with me a fortnight ago, heartbroken about you. I promised to make another attempt to find you, and I've just been to the B . . . Homes. Why did you leave there?'

"He had no answer, but I could see this well-built, still fine-looking man quivering with shame and emotion.

"We could not remain there with the crowd surging all about us, so I suggested a cup of tea in a nearby restaurant. He eagerly agreed, and soon gave evidence that more than a 'cup of tea' was needed. He had obviously been some time without adequate food.

"He had seen me pass his 'pitch' on a previous occasion and had hoped I would not recognise him in his strange attire, which was the property of his employer, and for which he had to pay for 'hiring' out of the few shillings taken each day. After paying this and the value of the stock sold, he often had barely sufficient to pay for his night's shelter and a little food. Yet with those few pence he gambled—and lost."

My recital of this man's story was evidently gripping the doctor's attention, for he was more than ordinarily interested, urging me to proceed.

"I must tell you that some months earlier a woman and her

child had been sent to me for guidance and help concerning the desertion by the husband of the woman and father of her child.

"It was a very pitiful story, similar in many respects to so many to which one has listened, but with one great difference.

"This man had been born into a godly family. His father had spent many years of his life as a preacher of the Gospel, had built up a Christian home and was a highly gifted and much-respected leader in the town where he was born. He and his excellent wife were keen not only to train their four children as Christians, but also to provide them with true education and opportunities for a useful and happy future.

"Great sacrifices had been made to attain these privileges, and the young people responded in a most promising way.

"There were two girls and two boys, all of whom gave great promise for the future.

"The eldest lad qualified for a medical career. The two girls became in turn outstanding teachers in their respective spheres. All were devoted to their parents.

"The youngest boy also gave evidence of success, and to his future his mother especially looked for a fine achievement.

"But this vision and hope were dimmed one day when a letter from his college brought a message which shocked the parents.

"They had earlier questioned the young fellow's choice of associates and had advised more care in his making acquaintances.

"But they had no definite knowledge of how far the influences of evil had affected this boy until this letter reached them.

"It revealed facts which meant that he was to be sent down in ignominy. After repeated warnings by those in authority, he had now been arrested with others involved in a disgraceful affair, and might be sent to prison.

"Evidently the offence was the result of a drunken orgy of such a character that it brought shame to all concerned. There was no way of preventing publicity, nor could the parents in any way intervene to save the offender from serious consequences.

"The blow fell, and the young man, whose prospects had been so bright, was sentenced to a term of imprisonment.

"He left the gaol an embittered and resentful individual, without any regard to the families to whom he had brought disgrace.

The drinking habit persisted, and after a few months, during which both mother and father died, he vanished from the old district and ceased to communicate with his sisters and brother.

"But one of his earlier friends, a girl who had been his great companion and admirer, having become a keen Christian herself, began to seek for him. She obtained knowledge of his whereabouts and met him.

"For a time he responded to her influence, and gained her good favour sufficiently to induce her to marry him. He was sufficiently trained to secure employment as a dispenser, and actually qualified by diligent study.

"Several years thus passed and a child was born to them. Then one day, the wife having suspected on several occasions that her husband had broken his promise never to take strong drink again, reproved him for doing so.

"At first he denied it, but later admitted that he had met some of his old friends, who had prevailed upon him to celebrate some occasion.

"That was not entirely true, for he had already been secretly dabbling with it when he did actually meet those others, and so was an easy victim.

"Soon it was evident that the craving for drink had seized him. He was reprimanded by his employer, angrily resented it, quarrelled and was dismissed.

"For a time his wife managed to maintain the home, then the fruitless struggle to find employment proved too much for him and again he disappeared, deserting his wife and child.

"All this I heard from the woman who sought my help to find her husband, and when, after a long search, he was traced, he confirmed the story and admitted his own wickedness.

"But the drink-habit was still his master. He was in poverty and in ill-health, full of remorse, yet unwilling to seek the only power which could enable him to overcome his craving."

While I was relating this part of the story, I observed my listener closely.

It was more than interesting to him. There was a growing eagerness. At length he interrupted with a question.

"What do you mean, Padre, by the only power?"

"I mean exactly what I said. I know of only one way in which the awful craving for drink, or any other besetting bad habit, can be really and finally overcome. I mean that I do know of a spiritual Power—a Person—Who can enable the weakest of us to become strong."

"You say a Person; and, of course, you mean Jesus Christ."

"I do!"

He sat with his hands covering his face, and I waited for his next words.

They were a long time coming. Then he looked up at me again, almost piteously.

"You do not know how you have been torturing me, Padre. I little dreamed when you began your story of Mr. S . . . that I should be involved in it, but it is so, and I must tell you how."

"You mean that you know S . . .?"

"I should never have recognised him, although, of course, the name should have reminded me, but I was in his year at Coll. I recall the happening which was so disgraceful; and at the time I fear that I was among those who derided religion and scoffed at parsons. But tell me the rest of the story and how S . . . became the man he now obviously is."

"Only too gladly, Doc. I perceive that it may mean much to you."

I continued: "I was telling you of our meeting again on Ludgate Hill and of our talk over a cup of tea and some food. It was then and there that conviction came to him as I read to him from my New Testament the words of Christ."

"What was it you read to him, Padre?" the doctor asked eagerly.

"It was that story in the third chapter of St. John: the story of a man who was so afraid of being seen talking with Jesus that he came, apparently surreptitiously, by night, and was told that the only way to get right with God was to be born again. Do you recall that story?"

"Yes, I do."

"Well, as I was quietly reading that passage I saw tears filling the eyes of the man opposite, and knew that conscience was being awakened. I prayed earnestly that God would make known to him the full meaning of the later words in that chapter—the great central truth of the Gospel in St. John, chapter three and verse sixteen."

As I quoted this verse I saw my doctor friend was greatly affected. After a pause he raised his face and laying his hand upon mine he said:

"I've never accepted that as including myself, but I do now. Will you pray with me?"

We knelt and prayed. They were tense moments. Once again, in His own remarkable way, my Lord had found another straying sheep who was to become in his own witnessing a "fisher of men".

"But," said he, "go on with the story of S . . ."

"When S . . . had finished his meal, in the silence which followed my reading, and we had left the café, he walked with me along Fleet Street to the Temple Gardens, where, on one of the seats, he made his confession of repentance and belief.

"It was not long before we were on our way to a quiet little street near Victoria Park where a faithful woman and her little son were surprised by two unexpected visitors—one in a strange costume, and the other a parson.

"It was an unforgettable scene.

"All the little woman said at first was, 'I knew you would come.' You see, Doctor, she had been all the time praying that someone would find S . . . That Someone was the Lord Jesus, but He needed human co-operation in His search, 'until He find it'.

"We had a wonderful hour in that humble home. The boy's part in it was just to sit silently holding his daddy's hand, and looking questioningly into his daddy's face, as if to say, 'You'll not go away again, Daddy?'

"Since then much has happened, Doctor. You'll remember the day S . . . was appointed here, now over a year ago, when he was selected from a number of applicants because of his earlier training and the excellent reference he had from his late employer's drug stores?"

"Yes, I do. And I also recall that the Chairman expressed his opinion that the new member of the staff would be an influence for good in the institution. How true that was to be we now know—thank God!"

The fervour of those last two words is with me as I now record this story.

Soon it was evident that there was a new and far-reaching influence at work in that place, for it was felt not only by the staff, but by many of the patients who bore witness to its reality.

Does the way in which the Lord brings together people for whom He seeks seem almost incredible?

If so, why?

Is He not Almighty? And being so, there is nothing in human affairs beyond His knowledge and His power.

Our incredulity, so often due to our own consciousness that we are wilful and disobedient, thus hindering His wise and loving plans, is in the way.

We go on admitting that it is so, repeating again and again that "We have left undone those things which we ought to have done, and we have done those things which we ought not to have done"; whereas, if the reverse had been true, we should have found that in still more wondrous ways "All things work together for good to those who love God."

Three

For the love of God is broader
Than the measure of man's mind,
And the heart of the Eternal
Is most wonderfully kind.

IT is very remarkable that words uttered in love for God, and with the desire to proclaim His Truth, are interpreted by hearers in divers ways. God's own Spirit applies to each hearer the meaning which he can best comprehend and use. One has often discovered this, and has been surprised to learn how much more precious use was made of simple words spoken than the speaker could imagine.

I was addressing a public meeting in Cardiff one day; and, observing in the audience one man of colour with a beaming countenance, asked a friend sitting at my side who he was.

"Oh, that's Happy Joe!" was his reply; and in a few whispered sentences he explained that a year previous Joe was of such a desperately violent character that it frequently required several policemen to carry him to the police cells. I could well imagine that to be true, for Joe was a big, burly fellow, who looked as if he were physically very strong. My personal knowledge of such as he enabled me to realise what he would be like when drunk. After the meeting I greeted him as we parted with the assembled friends, and noted that he was still apparently enjoying something unusually pleasing.

The next morning, which was Sunday, in company with the missioner's wife, I was walking homeward from church, and turning into Angelina Street, one of the numerous narrow streets forming that part of the port known as Tiger Bay, we saw ahead of us the massive form of Happy Joe, proceeding in the same direction. He was walking in the middle of the roadway, and every few seconds little children, who a year ago would have run away from him in terror, crept toward him shyly, took his hand, received from him a pat on the head or cheek, and then ran back into the houses where they lived, telling someone inside with delight, "I've seen Happy Joe." We watched this happening until we overtook him; and when I greeted him with "Good morning, Happy Joe! How are you this morning?" he swung round to face us and, recognising me, immediately burst into a laugh as he said:

"Good mornin', sah! You do make I larf!"

"Do I? Why do I make you laugh, Joe? Do I look comical?"

His face became very serious as he replied—and there was a profound expression in his manner and tone:

"Sah! You did say la' night, 'S'pose old Itler, s'pose ole Mushlini, s'pose ole Franco, s'pose ole Chamberlin all began to lub one anoder, wouldn't it be fine!'" And his solemn manner broke into another roar of laughter which brought other children out to see the cause.

Although those exact words were not mine, I saw that what had actually been said meant those things to this dark-skinned brother. He had caught the idea that if the love of which I had been speaking could fill the hearts of those national leaders, it would make a stupendous difference to the world. That was the substance of his subsequent enlargement upon this theme. He had been thinking it out, and had concluded that all the world really needed to bring international peace was such love between the peoples. And he is right; for however we may dress it up in fine phrases or avoid its implications, this is the one and only way to a happy settlement of human affairs.

If by some means there could be a change of procedure; if instead of suspicion, jealousy and hatred, men in authority could think lovingly, trustfully and generously of one another, there would be a halt in the mad race for supremacy in armaments.

The touch of a loving hand is really more potent than "scraps of paper" which can be ignored at will and are the cause of further contentions.

But how could such a desirable condition be brought about?

That has been the problem of the ages. It was that desire in the heart of God which made our fellowship in Christ a glorious possibility. "God so loved the world" and so desired those in the world to "love one another" "that He sent His only begotten Son into the world that whosoever believeth [every one who trusts] in Him should not perish, but have eternal Life." Yet, in spite of the fact that there are millions who say they trust in Him, we are still at strife, and manufacturing at headlong speed the most murderous weapons modern skill can devise to cause destruction and torture to each other. We are still permitting, in this enlightened Christian age, filthy literature and pictures to poison at its source the stream of young life upon which we say we depend to make a better world. The spirit of unrighteous gambling and greed was never so active and rampant as today. The craze for speed and gain is such that we kill and maim upon the public highways tens of thousands every year. We are so "air-minded" that it does not seem to matter that the peace and rest of our countryside on a Sabbath day are destroyed by the groaning of engines deafening and devastating. We are burrowing in tunnels and shelters and dug-outs so that at a given moment we may all scuttle like rabbits and worms from the surface of the earth, whereon we were intended to dwell together in peace and concord. Our cleverest chemists and scientists are busily engaged in inventing and manufacturing huge quantities of the most deadly and agonising poisons and gases, at the same moment that they are also endeavouring to discover the means of alleviating suffering. The mad folly of it!

We know that the consumption of alcoholic liquors fills our asylums and prisons and hospitals, yet we allow those who profit by the sale of these poisonous liquors to blatantly fill the hoardings and newspapers with the most astounding lies to deceive the youth of our time, and as they themselves express it, to "create a beer-minded youth" by pure deception. Pessimism? No! Truth, and we know it. The facts are all about us. Yet we go on uttering our prayers to Him Whose Name is Love. Yet His wonderful mercy is such that the fate of Sodom and Gomorrah is still not ours. Yet the Christ of Love still seeks His one wandering sheep and finds through human agency such as will elieve and, amidst all this insensate and depraved human folly nd sin, find a "Way" of tenderness and peace.

Happy Joe accompanied us as we journeyed, and told me of his udden conversion. At least, he said it was "all of a sudden". s he spoke of all that had preceded it, of the various persons and nfluences with which he had been brought into contact, I could iscern that the Lord had been following this coloured brother, eeking by many inscrutable means to win his hard heart. "I will how you where the dear Lord met me," he said as he led me to house in this same Angelina Street. Two small houses had been tructurally altered to form a mission centre run by the Christian ommunity, whose headquarters are in London. It was in the pstairs room, on one of the back seats, to which Joe led us, that ne night he responded to Christ's truth.

"It was in dat dere chair, sah, dat Joe met de Lord Who makes im so happy."

What a change had been wrought, where it had for so long eemed absurdly impossible. As I listened to his recital, while ears of joy welled in his eyes, I found myself being "strangely noved" in deep gratitude, for I knew only too well, from much xperience of this quarter of Cardiff city, what a hold Satan has pon those who dwell there. From all parts of the world seamen ome there to lodge with the kind of evildoer who soon relieves hem of whatever they possess, and leads them into all manner f wickedness. It seems that in this wilderness of a place, so full f the inevitable misery and degradation consequent upon such rocedure, even in this place God still uses human hands and uman hearts to heal the sin-sick who will turn to Him.

I have learnt much more about my friend Joe since that day. here are men from far-away parts of the world who have told ne that it was his happy testimony which led them to "think pon their ways" and turn to Christ for pardon and peace. Joe n his simple and unphilosophic way bore his testimony "in eason, out of season", by the wayside, in the ship's fo'c'sle or ngine-room, along the quayside in foreign ports, amid the torms at sea, or amid the crowds in market-places, and always eft the picture of a "healed man", which seeing, no man could ispute.

He was so doing when the ship in which he was sailing wa
sunk by enemy action. When the whole story is related I know
that we shall hear that, in the hour of their desperate testing, thi
man gave supreme and final evidence of his love for Jesus an
his fellow men.

Four

Ask the Saviour to help you,
Comfort, strengthen and keep you;
He is willing to aid you;
He will carry you through.

IT was one of those days when events and claims crowded so thickly that, but for the continuous remembrance that our work is Divinely guided, we should be harassed and weakened. Ordinary physical and mental ability had been taxed to its utmost, and every possible reserve had been called up. It would have been very easy, and seemingly justifiable, to turn aside from a request for further service. The body and the mind were tired and reaching the point of exhaustion. Meeting the diverse and intricate problems of others, entering into the complexities of tangled lives hitherto strange to the listener, tendering advice and help to those sadly needing understanding friends, yet again and again failing to fit the need because of some still more perplexing aspect left unrevealed until now—all this is very wearing. Yet how patiently, how tenderly God deals with us all! He gives us the unerring guidance of His Spirit, and in ways past our understanding He suggests lines of approach and guidance most wonderfully effective and startling in their results.

As we turned aside thoughtfully from what we imagined to be our last interview one evening, preparing as we walked the notes roughly made for later consideration, having bidden God-speed to the couple who, an hour before, had met us with despairing hearts, but now departed to "do what God tells us", there appeared a man with a timid request, "Could you spare me a moment, sir?"

A glance at his face was sufficient to discover that here was another whose need was great.

He could be immediately classified. A "down and out"; a drunkard; physically exhausted; mentally distracted; suffering intensely from the results of folly; trembling as he stood; endeavouring to steady himself for a conversation with a new personality; bearing all the marks of recent debauchery; and appearing to have been just cleaned up, possibly in a hospital or prison. So I rapidly concluded.

"Yes, laddie! What can I do for you?"

As my eyes met his for a moment his glance fell. He seemed to find difficulty in answering my question. I waited.

"Sir—thank you for not refusing me. May I come in and talk with you? I need a friend."

We proceeded to a quiet room, and he sat wearily down on the seat I had indicated.

"Well! Can I be your friend?" I asked, as kindly as I could.

He looked up at me with a pitiful gaze and held out his hand toward me in a dazed way, as if he wished me to take it.

I did so, and realised his extremely urgent need at once. He was a very sick man.

"Drink!" was all he said as we held hands, his trembling violently in mine.

I needed no telling. The ghastly fact was writ large. I could almost hear the fiendish laugh of the Evil One who had led and ruined this poor soul. Also, I needed no telling, as in those few silent moments I recalled the rushing volume of similar stories that were obviously to be repeated. Probably differing in detail, but so alike in general tenor. I felt that I could almost begin his story for him and fill in much of the detail also, but I waited for his recital, as I claimed once again the aid of the Lord to instruct us how to deal with, and bring back, this wanderer.

Then he suddenly stood up and burst out, his eyes flashing dangerously, his fists clenched:

"Why don't you fling me out? I'm done for. I'm not worth helping. I've flung everything away. I'm a filthy beast. Put me back in the asylum. Send me to prison. Thrash me! Spurn me! Kill me! Don't look at me like that; I'm not worth it."

So he went on for a minute or two, and I just let him do so.

"That's all true," I said quietly—"very true; but it is not all the story. There is something more to be said about it. I know a good deal about you, but I'm first going to ask you why you came here?"

"I came here as a last hope. Not that there is any for me. But since I'm hungry for food, and hungrier still for a bit of friendship, I promised a chap I met, a stranger to me, that I'd call and see you. He told me that you helped fellows like me, though he didn't know how helpless I am. But I came, and now you've seen me and heard my ravings you can but tell me to go. I'm used to that."

"What do you mean by saying you are used to it?"

"Used to being told to clear out; told to mend my ways; told I'm no good and fit only for the company of such as myself."

"Who told you that?"

"Everybody: my own folk; people in London here who talk about the Almighty on Sundays and forget Him all the week; preachers who don't believe what they preach; officials who are supposed to help men who need food and shelter and put them on their feet. On their feet! I oughtn't to talk like that. I've been trying to stand on my head. I'm mad! I know I'm mad. I've been in three asylums. I've had D.T.s. I've got it now. I can't keep still. I hate drink, but I want some more. Give me a few coppers to get a drink!"

Again I had let him rave on, quietly waiting for a pause during which I might say a word to help. He was now glaring at me with a dangerous, menacing look. Then he would stare away beyond me as if seeing something or somebody not visible to me. He was devil-possessed. Alternately, he would laugh and cry, whimpering like a child, trembling in every limb. I could see that the excitement of his attempt to make known to me his own state was driving him in the wrong direction.

"Look! Can't you see that devil after me? He's been there for weeks: everywhere I go he follows and mocks like that at me. Hide me, will you? Mind, there's another! More of them! Hold me! No! Let me get at them. I'll smash them." And he lunged and plunged across the room, frantically punching out at imaginary forms which none could see but himself.

I did not try to restrain him: it would be useless, and possibly make matters worse. Presently he grew quiet again and sank into a seat, with his head and arms upon the table. It was a terrible sight, but alas, all too familiar. Often had we seen similar episodes in that room. Men, aye and women too, "in God's image", yet so degraded and in such bondage that the Devil was leading them captive at his will.

For some moments we remained thus. Then, kneeling by his side and holding his hand, I called upon our Father to help us in guiding this lost soul into His way. It was not difficult to pray. The Lord Himself was there, more desirous, more eager than I to save. As I interceded I heard words, dear familiar words of promise and pleading, of pleading and promise, reiterated again and again. "Come unto Me . . . and I will give . . ." I prayed very earnestly that my brother man might hear them too. That the same Spirit, Who was "bringing to my remembrance" the other promise that "greater things than these shall ye see", might break down the power of evil in this man's heart, might restore even the physical temple which was marred and broken, so that hearing and perception might become active once more, unhindered by the hallucinations which had controlled them.

I lost sense of everything save that I was engaged in a life-and-death struggle for a soul. Time did not matter. Physical inconvenience was not present. I did hear a key turned in the door-lock, the door opened and quietly shut again, but for possibly half an hour or more we were left undisturbed. Then I became aware that he had lifted his head and was looking at me, and as I raised my eyes to his, he began to cry, not in the whimpering manner of an hour ago, but in penitence. His hands, which had been for some time gripping mine, relaxed their hold, and I then became conscious that my hands were aching from the unusual gripping and bore marks as from blows. He saw it too, and with a sound which was almost a groan he sought to rub away the marks. Then he spoke, and I knew that the thing for which Jesus died had been accomplished. The power of the Devil was broken, and this soul set free as in old time. The evil spirit was "cast out" and would leave the man "for a season".

"Sir—can you forgive me?"

"It's not for me to do that. Only One has that power," I replied.

"I know what you mean, but I've hurt you."

"You've hurt Him more."

"I know that too, and if I could feel more sure of myself, I'd ask His forgiveness. But you see, sir, I've thrown away my claim to His forgiveness. I'm beyond the pale. I am a physical as well as a spiritual wreck. I knew the way of God's salvation and have wilfully spurned it. He has had great mercy, and I've sinned beyond His reach. While you were praying I tried to pray and couldn't. I knew what I wanted to say, but hadn't the power. I knew God was here, but I deserve no pity from Him. I've said so many times I had no room for Him. I only wanted my fling and then to die. But, God help me, now I'm afraid to die. My hell is already prepared. I've tasted it. Tried to escape it. Found myself sinking lower and lower into it, until I was mad, mad; but while you were praying I seemed to come to myself again. I heard words I used to read as a boy in Sunday School—words I've heard from preachers and have scorned. It seemed as if God were trying to reach me, to touch me. It seemed as if your hands were the hands of Christ trying to hold me. I wanted them to do so, but something in me made me afraid of letting Him do so. Then I saw that I had hurt your hands, and somehow it hurt me. Those marks remind me of something else."

"Thank God!" I almost shouted. "Thank God!"

He looked awakened, and as I paused he waited.

"Yes, thank God! For if you have been reminded that our Saviour's hands were hurt for you, it will soon be easy for you to realise more than that. His heart was broken for you! But He lives also for you, and is here now, waiting to freely forgive everything and make you His Father's son."

"Me?"

"Yes, laddie, even you! Come, let Him heal. He is the Great Physician, and you've only to turn from the sin which has hitherto mastered you and seek His pardon for it, and in that moment He will give you power to beat the Evil One. Will you?"

This page will be read possibly in all kinds of places, and by readers with all kinds of experiences and circumstances. It may be difficult to visualise the scene I have just tried to recall. That is one of the great differences between the personal relation of facts when from one personality to another there is conveyed the full reality of experiences, when by gesture, tone and inflection of voice one can so describe the happenings that the hearer almost witnesses their recurrence; but in cold print, maybe in a noisy vehicle, in a comfortable chair, seated in a garden or library, or with a sense of other comfortable influences around one, it is not so easy to perceive the reality of the scene depicted, nor to enter into the spiritual realisation of the event. Yet I have known frequently that this is possible, and I pray that when the reader has read thus far he will endeavour to detach himself from the immediate environment, whatever it may be, and read on in a separated manner the remainder of this story. The real world is not the material one. The mind which is now interpreting these words, in whatever language they may be printed—that mind is the "you" to whom the words are addressed;—that spirit which is yours is the only real possible contacting element with God Who made it. He witnesses with our spirit when we liberate ourselves from our material surroundings. Our bodies are the houses—"temples"—in which we live temporarily: but our spirits—we—are bigger, more wonderful, more free to commune with God if we forget the bodies and dwell in heavenly places with Him. Therefore get near to God and pray for others who may be needing the touch of a loving hand to save them.

The man sitting by my side was hearing words which I could not hear. In my human way I was endeavouring to influence him to make a decision. In His Divine way my Lord was revealing Himself as the only Saviour and Redeemer. The man's wayward spirit was being challenged as never before, and the challenge must be dealt with. What could he do? Pitifully he looked in my direction for help. I had none to give him beyond my own desperately earnest desire to save him. But help came. Slowly I saw returning a recognition of the meaning of the present incidents. He had been led to this moment in order to determine his future course. He must choose this offer of Christ's pardon and love or——!

In words all he said was "I will"; but slipping from his chair, he dropped on his knees beside me, and for some moments we were both silent. Then he stood. He took my hands again and, looking at them intently, he began a brief statement which I will not try to report here. It was a trembling, halting, but gladdening sentence or two which convinced me that he had become a "new creature"; that "old things had passed away"; and that his future would be governed by "What would Jesus have me do?"

Since that day those who know my friend have witnessed in him such a transformation that they can only describe as "wonderful".

It is not only that he has been changed from a degraded wretch into a respectable citizen, from a physical wreck into an upstanding figure of healthy manhood, from moral depravity to a life of rectitude, but his whole character and outlook on life have been transformed. He is gentle and kind and generous, instead of bitter and hard and selfish. In his dealings with his fellow men, I find constantly that he sees the best in them, views them from the "brother" standpoint and is full of desire to help them in the way he himself has been helped. As he puts it: "I know Who saved and Who keeps me, and I want everybody to know Him as I do."

This man has, I am certain, a wide ministry in the future years. His quiet influence is already affecting quite a number of folk who are not yet in a position spiritually wherein they would readily admit the fact. So many people are like that. Their lives are being blessed through another's Christian discipleship; they are following good examples and finding joy therein, but they do not add their witness to Christ's saving and keeping power.

Five

"*Joy shall be in Heaven over one sinner that repenteth.*" (Luke xv, 7.)

"*He is able!*"

WE had been marching through the narrow streets and alleys of our "parish" just east of Aldgate, but nearer the River Thames, with its sordid fringe of warehouses, docks, slums and hovels, announcing the fact that at 11.30 p.m. on the last day of the year we should be holding a Watch-night Service, to observe the passing of another year, to thank God for all His mercies and to resolve that by His help we would make the New Year a better one by our living more consistently and righteously. Those two words were doubtless the subject of much criticism, if not abuse, for on our march we had halted outside many of the undesirable and well-known drinking dens, and had not failed to make strong attacks upon the normal proceedings within, with references also to the tragic results in the surrounding "homes".

We lived in the midst of them, and we knew.

Our last halt was near one of the most infamous of such places. Often one had visited this vile place to reach someone who needed such personal attention, and had sometimes been successful in persuading a client—victim would be a better word—to leave the premises either to go home, to come to our services, or, in some early morning instances, to go to his employment, knowing that having left home with that intent the man had been waylaid or beguiled just to "have one" en route, and the "one" had led to further lingering likely to result in loss of employment and suffering in the family.

Often the landlord had asked me facetiously if I couldn't "mind my own business".

The poor fellow could not perceive that this was precisely what I was doing—minding "my Father's business", which is also mine.

Our procession had passed on to the Mission, having fulfilled its purpose, while I entered to seek any who might be prevailed upon to come with us.

Three men were in the bar, only one of whom I knew.

Harry —— lived nearby in one of the blocks of dwellings which comprised the more respectable area—although much tragedy abounded therein. His two companions were not local inhabitants, but were "casuals" such as abounded in that part of Dockland.

I perceived that they were of the scrounging type and had already succeeded in relieving Harry of his money. He was well on the way to being drunk, and in such condition was easily persuaded to have "another", for which apparently he had just paid and saw that his "friend" had gathered up the change and was pocketing it.

I fear that my appearance interrupted his remonstrances and surprised him so much that he forgot to pursue his claim to his own.

As I appealed to him to come along with me, his companions hilariously teased him about his parson friend, and I saw that while he was somewhat abashed at being found in such a state, he was not ready to accede to my persuading.

Then the taunting turned to coarse abuse which I could not openly resent, so had to leave Harry to ponder my words of reproach.

Just as I was nearing the door, one of the men shouted, "Chuck it over him!" and before I could escape, the pots of beer were hurled at me, and one of them caught the side of my face, grazing it rather badly. The liquor had drenched my head and shoulders, and I had to be cleaned up a bit before commencing the service.

None of my people had witnessed the affair, but two were just coming to see why I had been delayed, and were not altogether surprised, for similar things had occurred on other occasions.

We had a great crowd in the large Hall for the service. This was not unusual, for there was each year then a widespread idea that in some special way the Almighty would be placated by the spending of the last few minutes in church and by the attendance there for the commencement of a New Year.

For the Christians it was an opportunity to renew their good resolutions, and possibly lead "outsiders" to begin attending a place of worship. So they came in goodly numbers.

Instructions had been given that the doors be closed at two minutes to twelve o'clock, in order that there should be no interruption of the last "one-minute silence". This was observed and my appeal for decisions had been made.

Then, before I could announce the closing hymn, there was a movement among the people at the rear of the meeting and some score of men and women walked down the aisle. First among them was Harry. Somewhat unsteadily, but resolutely, he came forward and, turning, he addressed those who were following.

His first words were of deep regret and apology for what had happened, and then:

"God helping me, I'll never touch another drop as long as I live."

Falling to his knees, he could be heard sobbing; and I knew that God was answering the few words of prayer I had uttered on my way to the service that God would, in His mercy and for Jesus' sake, save the soul of this man. He did!

Day by day we saw a reconstruction of that life.

Owing to long military service he had been given employment at the Tower of London, where every day his duties brought him into contact with many visitors to that historic place. He did not fail to use such opportunities for witnessing, and, moreover, his fellow-workers in that place saw a transformation such as could scarcely be believed.

Harry had, however, to bear a very heavy cross. His wife was also a drink-addict and in her case all approaches seemed to fail to bring her to Christ. Again and again effort was made. We saw the home going literally to pieces.

Even Harry's clothing was sold or pawned to obtain drink; but although he had to attend in his working attire, he would not fail to be in his place. More than once we had to press him to tell us why this happened, and we marvelled at the tender patience with which he reluctantly explained. Then he would say, with an expression of gracious pity:

"You see, I taught her to drink! She did not take it at all when we married, but I persuaded her; and now I must suffer with her until, please God, she sees as I do that the power of Christ is the only one that can enable her to conquer!"

Then with a bright flash in his eyes he would say:

"But I know it can—and will."

Long after I had left that neighbourhood I learned that the victory was won—but only just, for she was taken soon after to meet again the One Who had stood by her in her great battle.

Six

"We touch Him in life's throng and press,
And we are whole again."

SEATED in one of London's crowded underground trains, watching with deep interest the frequently changing passengers, I wondered whether among those struggling to emerge at each station or among those who were fortunate enough to find entrance, there might be one whom I had been seeking.

So far there had been no such discovery.

But at one of the stopping places during the scrimmage at the door, my attention was attracted by a man who had contrived to get quickly through the crowd and hastily occupy the only available seat by my side.

He was in rags, and I detected the all-too-familiar odour which told me much about his habits and probable lodging-places by night. This unsavoury condition may have accounted for the speedy entrance through the crowd at the door.

I also noticed another man of a very different type entering, well dressed, and of genial appearance, wearing a flower in his jacket lapel. I did not see where he found room, owing to the fact that our long double compartment was so densely packed from end to end.

But the man on my right had, I felt sure, been sent that I might in some way befriend him. He was dejected and so obviously a "lost sheep", and I an "ambassador for Christ". Yet to speak to him under the existing conditions was physically impossible, for the standing strap-hangers crowded so upon us that no such converse could take place.

But I could speak with my God, and was led to think that it would be best to await the possibility of his leaving the train at another station soon.

This happened a couple of stations later, and I followed him out. But again he was permitted to pass through the struggling crowd more quickly than I, and I feared he might elude me. On to the rising escalator he hurried, but not before I had just time to reach him and say:

"You are in trouble, friend. Can I help you in any way?"

He angrily replied as he hastened on:

"Yes! I'm in trouble, but I want none of your help."

How grateful I was and am that his rude rejection was disregarded!

When I reached the top of the escalator, there he stood awaiting me. The wonder-working "Seeker" had intervened once again.

"Did you mean what you said just now, sir?" he asked as I appeared.

"Of course I did. What can I do to help you?"

"Get me something to eat. I'm hungry, very hungry."

"That can be managed. Come along!"

Out into Oxford Street we hastened, and soon found a place to obtain food, sat at a table, and I noted with what eagerness he attacked the food brought to us. Often I have been asked for money to buy food when it was not really sought for that purpose; but this man was really hungry. I noted the obviously resentful interest we aroused as we took our seats, and the waitress who served us did not disguise her disdain; but did I also discern here and there evidence of sympathy and pity?

I knew One was there, "the Man of Sorrows acquainted with grief", and I heard His whisper: "Inasmuch as ye did it unto one of the least of these My brethren ye did it unto Me." Since my companion was evidently needing the food provided, I did not at once talk to him, but presently produced my pocket Testament. He observed it and listened as I recited to him some of its message. Then, quietly laying aside his knife and fork, he said:

"That's what I need, sir. I need that Saviour."

"Thank God you know that; but finish your food and we'll go outside and tell Him so."

He did not take long to complete his meal, and we left the building. I intended to take him along to the nearby park, where there was a seat which had sometimes been a "sanctuary" under similar conditions. But as we walked I became conscious that another was keeping step with us.

There was of course One with us, as He promised.

But as I glanced to my left I saw the tall man with the flower in his coat whom I had noticed in the train. He caught my inquiring glance and said:

"Yes, sir, it is I. I saw him sitting next to you in the train, and that you were interested in him. I felt sure you would speak to him. I was also sitting near you in the café and heard some of the things you said to him. But, sir, if any man in London needs the Saviour of Whom you spoke, I am that man."

To say that I was thrilled is inadequately to express my emotion.

"This is grand," I replied. "We are just going to a quieter spot in the park. Will you come with us?"

"Gladly, sir; but I do not think you are really aware of what is happening."

This saying caused me some prayerful reflection as we proceeded, for one has experienced such astonishing evidences of God's power and love which no merely human ingenuity could plan nor conceive. What did he mean? Only He Who was guiding us fully knew. We could only pursue the prompting of His Holy Spirit; so on to the park seat we went. Soon we three were on our knees confessing our sins and seeking forgiveness. I had the joy of hearing my two companions make sincere appeals individually and independently, but I had no idea of any related conditions.

After expressing my personal gratitude to God for the privilege that was mine and commending my brethren to Him in their apparently so diverse circumstances, we resumed our seats, I greatly wondering what the many passers-by had thought of the unusual scene.

As the two men were about to shake hands I said:

"This is a great and wonderful occasion; and although we are all strangers to each other, I must ask you to tell me how I can continue to communicate in order to further help if possible."

Our friend with the flower in his coat was the first to reply. "You need not ask him his name," he said, referring to the man in rags. "Your name is ——, isn't it?"

"Yes! That's my name; but how do you know it? Who are you?"

Without replying, the tall man took from his pocket a card-case from which he extracted a nicely printed card which he handed to me. It bore a name and beneath it, "Managing Director" and the name of a suburban firm in the west of London.

I passed the card to the other man, who stared first at it and then at our tall friend, exclaiming "Good God!"

I, too, was naturally astonished; and in response to my looks of silent inquiry, I learned that years ago the man in rags had been the employer of the other. One had prospered in material ways; the other had gone down, down, until today when he begged for food. Yet, as the business man made it clear, both were equally prodigals; for sin in insidious forms had still been ruling in his heart until this providential meeting. I found that even amidst his busy and outwardly prosperous life he had been guilty of duplicity and utter selfishness, which threatened to destroy his business reputation and to break up a lovely home and family.

Neither of them knew me until that day, but the Saviour now accepting them had led us thus to meet that He might make "all things new".

In that business house, where in a very short time the man who had begged for bread was installed as a trusted worker, there was formed a Christian Union, having as its chairman and leader the Managing Director, and as its Secretary the man who "wanted none of my help".

It has been my great privilege to visit that gathering and address the employees, who, unconscious of the above details, yet know that the Christ of Whom I spoke is the "Head of that house"—as He is the Head of the happy home of their Director, to which many of them have been invited on occasions to share in a "squash".

Seven

OUR welfare work is not without extraordinary and complicated difficulties. Only those who have graduated in the school of life can hope to be equal to the diverse problems which arise in the process of dealing with human poverty. It has been said that "Necessity is the mother of invention". Certainly it is true that many clever and cunning schemes to obtain money have been "invented" by persons in dire need; and here is the story of one such, related in the hope that publicity may prevent similar adventures.

Captain Z . . . first became known to me years ago when, owing to a domestic upheaval and consequent unemployment, he sought our aid at Headquarters. The details of this part of his story need not be enumerated here. Suffice it to say that he took to himself none of the blame for the fact that the family were divided into two very hostile camps, his own being very much in the minority. We confirmed the main facts, however, and decided to aid the seafarer in distress. Our personal contact with Z . . . left nothing to be desired. He was amiable, temperate, well-behaved, active in seeking re-employment.

After a prolonged search work was found and he left to join a ship. Unfortunately he entirely forgot to make any attempt to reimburse the Society's funds. But then, very few remember to do so. In this matter it seems to be true that "Sailors don't care", or—they forget. We will leave it at that—Z . . . forgot.

Towards the close of 1931 Captain Z . . . again visited Headquarters and was again in serious difficulties, as, alas, so many of his fellow officers are. We were not at all surprised when he told us that he had been out of a ship for a long time and at last had mustered sufficient boldness to seek help again from those who had befriended him before and to whom he was still indebted. We forgave the debt and accommodated him. In several conversations we elicited the fact that the old domestic strife continued and that, with one exception, all his family had—to use his own phrase—been turned against him. Be that as it may, we found him still the same typical sailor-man, kind-hearted, genial and apparently trustworthy.

True, there was just one item which caused the writer to keep one eye open.

A certain incident which resulted in dismissal from a ship was not satisfactorily explained. At any rate, there was some reserve of judgment in our minds on this point.

However, so fully had Z . . . won his way with all with whom he came in contact that he was asked to act as Father Christmas at our Christmas party. He entered into the fun of the thing, and was apparently so whole-heartedly intent upon helping in every way possible, that we cannot believe that, up to that time and for some weeks after, he had any intention to proceed upon the lines indicated by the remainder of this story.

One day he came to the office evidently well-pleased to inform us that temporary work had been offered by an old shipmate. This we confirmed, and the daily habits which followed were quite consistent with all we knew of the work he had obtained.

Naturally, after a time we began to ask how long this "temporary" employment was to last. Rather vague answers were at first given, but there seemed to be no tangible reason for new suspicions, until we noticed that Z . . . was obviously avoiding us.

We then made a very definite appointment for a personal interview, and this precipitated matters.

Now I know that Z . . . had for several weeks been quietly operating upon some of his fellow lodgers in a most plausible and deceptive way. Those whom he approached he bound down to the strictest secrecy by the suggestion that if it should leak out that he had this scheme on hand it would lead to the loss of the promised well-paid job.

A very high-class steam yacht was being prepared in a Scottish port for a world tour combining pleasure and business. She was to carry about fifty passengers, some of whom were named. They comprised wealthy and important persons who were prepared to pay high rates for a first-class trip. Captain Z . . . had been asked to take charge and to find his crew of "picked" men and stewardesses.

All had seemed fair to the "selected" men engaged by Captain Z . . ., and they loyally (but foolishly) told no one of their engagement.

It was not until we pressed for the definite appointment that any news leaked out. Naturally we were then suspicious. The scheme was now about to mature. The day had arrived. Z . . . saw us at 11 a.m. He admitted that he was embarking upon this grand scheme, but by four o'clock he would be free to divulge all the particulars.

Four o'clock arrived, and with it came Captain Z . . . He was well dressed, apparently very happy and still quietly self-restrained but confident. All was settled. He was leaving London for the North and was taking with him certain of the officers he had engaged, among them those who were concerned with the provisioning of the craft. He was accompanied to King's Cross to join the train, but no one knows whether he embarked or not. The engaged men awaited in vain the promised "wires" calling them to Scotland. No trace of such a vessel as Z . . . described could be found in a Scottish port. It had been carefully stated that the ship was American-owned and was to be renamed, so that no register could be searched. Many days have since passed, bringing no tidings of either Z . . . or the ship.

The tragedy of the case is deepened by the fact that several of the very worthy men who were "engaged" entered into contracts for special clothing and equipment and now find themselves in heavy debts with no chance of meeting them.

Where is Captain Z . . .?

We are taking every possible means to discover him and to find out what he has done with the sums of money he "borrowed" from his fellow officers who, to help him, themselves borrowed and had to repay.

Eight

AMONG the many hideouts, night clubs, hostels, common lodging-houses and other less desirable places to which my endeavours to "find" lost folk had called me was one known as "The Chambers" in Ratcliffe Highway, London E.1. "The Chambers" was owned and controlled by a remarkable man for whom I had real respect. "Charley", as he was known to those who frequented his rather extensive premises, was a real Cockney character combining shrewdness and generosity of a praiseworthy kind.

My story relates to this place, because it had become to me most interesting as a place of Christian adventure. There I had met remarkable people. My visits were always welcomed, and the proprietor was very friendly, helpful and respectful; never resentful of my attempts to talk with him on spiritual matters. He was indeed quite a character. Behind his apparent rough and hard appearance there was a kind and generous disposition. He was a friend to many a prodigal who applied for a "kip", being without the means to pay the small cost thereof. To such Charley was often a Good Samaritan. Naturally quick-witted, with a keen sense of humour, he had also become through his long experience a quite good judge of character. There were some regulars who had lodged with Charley for years, but there were some who never dared enter "The Chambers" again for various reasons.

As I say, many a down-and-out found in Charley a real friend, and often when I visited "The Chambers" he would consult me concerning one or other of his guests. Thus it came to pass that one day he said:

"There's a chap here I'd like you to talk to. He's a bit queer, but seems a decent fellow. He's just cooking his kipper at the stove, but I'd wait till he sits down at the table by the window, if I was you."

I looked in the direction indicated and saw a man whose

features seemed familiar, although I could not at once identify him. (There were several men cooking food at a huge glowing fire standing in the centre of the large apartment.)

"Why do you think I should speak to him?" I asked.

"Well, he's been coming here now and again, and has given me an idea that he's got a wife and some kids somewhere. Told me he used to booze a bit, but he's trying to quit it."

I decided to fulfil Charley's suggestion, and when the man moved to the seat mentioned, crossed the room to speak to him.

He was difficult. Each attempt to open up conversation was met by a stolid silence. But I was assured we had met before. When I hinted at this he suddenly left his seat and his partly consumed meal, made for the door and hurriedly disappeared.

"Did he give you any clue to the district he came from?" I asked Charley.

After a moment's thoughtful delay he said:

"Yes, he did mention one or two places, and he used to live near —— railway station."

Immediately there came to my mind Mac's story of his meeting with Joe on that amazing occasion related in the book "Lovest Thou Me?". Then it also occurred to me that not only was this man's appearance faintly familiar, but it could hardly be coincidence that the particular railway station near where they met should be thus mentioned. I hastened out into the street in the hope that I might overtake the man, but in the darkness found no trace.

Mac had become a highly respected worker at an office in the West End and lodged in North London. I wrote him telling him of the incident, and he replied informing me that in his search for Joe he had traced and made contact with the deserted wife and children. He had succeeded in persuading Joe's wife to give up drinking, had found her a dwelling and had enabled her to secure employment with the firm for whom he was working. That was excellent news, for which I praised God. He would renew his endeavours to find the husband, with God's help. He would come and see me soon, so that I could direct him to "The Chambers" and follow up the clue.

When he did so I was filled with deep gratitude to the Lord

for the most wonderful transformation in the man now sitting by my side. A "new creature" indeed! Not only in physical appearance, but in the deep spiritual experience evidenced in his conversation. He told me of the events following the never-to-be-forgotten scenes already recorded in my book and of the happy result. His humble acknowledgment of God's patience and mercy was sincerely and repeatedly expressed. His health had been completely restored. The introduction given him to the Christian Institution where he was now employed had brought him into a wealth of fellowship which had seemed lost to him for ever. His earlier training, experience and his abilities were now being used in his present employment. He was using every opportunity to reveal his love for God, and as he spoke of his daughter, his tear-filled eyes shone with joy. He had made many attempts to trace Joe, and regarded the news I had given him as an answer to prayer.

So the search began again. Together we visited "The Chambers", talked with Charley, who promised to advise me if the man to whom I had spoken ever returned there. Several weeks passed with no further development.

Then, as in so many instances, came another evidence that the Lord had been planning.

It transpired that, returning from one of his frequent journeys to visit the home of his daughter some miles out of London, Mac saw a group of outside porters at the railway station engaged in some dispute about the handling of baggage, one of whom reminded him of Joe. He made inquiries of an official concerning this man, but the name given him was not that of Joe. He therefore, still feeling that he was being guided, paid a later visit to the terminus and was fortunate in at once meeting the man, who proved indeed to be his missing friend. At first Joe resisted Mac's entreaty to "Come with me and see for yourself what has happened". He told Joe how he had himself become a Christian through the remarkable events related in "Lovest Thou Me?" and how he had traced the deserted wife and children and befriended them.

"They will not want to see me," Joe had said with bitterness.

But Mac, having himself proved the wonder-working power

of God's love in Christ, was not letting go. He persisted and prayerfully pleaded, until at last Joe promised to pray himself for forgiveness. An appointment was made for a further meeting, which took place at the men's hostel where Joe was then lodging. By the mercy of God, light came into Joe's darkened soul; and Mac's joy was unbounded as he realised that although all unworthy, he had been privileged to "find" a lost sheep for Christ.

A day or two later there was another reunion, for Joe was now more than willing to meet again those whom he had deserted. Arrangements were made with the friends whom Mac had persuaded to let their rooms to the woman and her children, for the husband to visit them. Indeed, these friends, being members of the local church which Mac had also joined, eagerly cooperated in the good work and made temporary provision for Joe to dwell there also.

I was invited to "Come and see what the Lord is doing for Joe and his family". The invitation was gladly accepted, and I learned over a cup of tea with them that although there did not appear to be any connection between the evident work of Grace and "The Chambers" in Ratcliffe Highway, it was really through that seeming casual request of Charley and my response that Joe was discovered by Mac. He had run away from "The Chambers" because he recognised me when I spoke to him, and, as he said, "was afraid you would talk to me about religion, so I decided to keep away from that place. Then I came up here to North London and dossed at a place where I met a man who talked to me about the railway, where I got a job as an outside porter," Thus he was led to the place and day when Mac identified him. Praise God!

Later another stage in God's plan for these good folk developed. "I know you'll be glad to see our new home," wrote Joe in sending me an invitation to visit them at a suburban house to which a name has been given. With them I found Mac, now "Uncle Mac", established as part of the family, living happily with "Christ as the Head of this house".

Nine

"AND lo I am with you alway, even unto the end"—that's just where we are failing as His ambassadors. Many either do not understand these words, or they forget them, or they ignore them. Hence there is an inquiry today as to whether the Gospel of Christ is still achieving results which followed the preaching of earlier witnesses!

I want to make the emphatic statement that not only is there no doubt about it, but also that, wherever the promise above quoted is realised, there can be no other result. To be with Him in conscious association is to undergo that kind of transformation at which beholders still marvel. "Mighty miracles" we are apt to call these things, yet they are only the natural sequence of faithfulness to Him.

Loving obedience to the words of Christ would transform even the mad world in which we live at this hour. The way to this universal transformation is obviously through the individual souls of men, and in this matter it is good to make inquiry. Does the Gospel work?

If half-a-century's experience of Christ's transforming power in the lives of men and women, and through them in the life of the community, may be acceptable as real evidence, I gladly answer Yes!

It is true to state that notwithstanding all the tremendous changes of thought and habit during that period, the human need remains the same and the Divine plan in all its simplicity abides.

This is true whether the circumstances be relative to the crowded slums of London and other great cities or to the remote glens and vales of the Highlands; the comfortable homes of the well-to-do white folk, or the tent dwellings of the coloured natives of Africa or India. Wherever the human heart turns to Christ, there He is to forgive and to transform. Nor can a single soul evade His quest. He seeks us out, and no place can hide us from

His Love. Prison walls cannot prevent Him, nor the vast spaces elude His searching eagerness to find us.

Elsewhere I have related many striking illustrations of these truths selected from the harvest of the years, and the very telling of them has brought a further reaping which is a constant inspiration. Here is one such which, as I write, is still being developed.

Many years ago a young couple quarrelled and parted. The man, hurt by deep resentment and bitter disappointment, went his way in a desperate mood to quench his feelings in a bout of reckless drinking. He went very deeply into every kind of wrongdoing. He formed evil associations which led all the while into grosser forms of sin and law-breaking. Prison held him again and again. He turned his hand against every man. Bitterness poisoned his spirit and many devils possessed him. About a year ago there happened events which I can only briefly relate, but which have changed entirely everything concerning him.

On his release from prison he determined to end his career by suicide. He would revisit the place where he last parted from the girl to whom he attributed his ruin. He would go to that cliff-top by the sea and finish his sorrow where it had begun.

He reached the old seat. Back to his mind came the old scene, and he was strengthened in his wrong intention by the flood of bitter memories. He would wait until darkness came, and then finish the life which had been such an utter failure.

For an hour he sat, thus growing mentally more and more miserable and desperate.

Then, "while he was yet a great way off", His Father saw him and in His own incredibly simple way sent His messenger. There "chanced" to walk in that direction one whom God has often used in that seaside town to carry His messages of love. He was out to enjoy an evening stroll up the hillside, and saw our ex-prisoner on the seat, which was really a place of peril in the dark, especially if one were unaccustomed to the place. He must be warned. So my friend approached the stranger with a friendly word of caution. It was at first resented. Then my friend's quiet and gentle mode of expression made its appeal. God's Spirit interpreted and reminded the desperate man of truth learned in his youth. Back in swift flashes came the words of God's Book, sharply reminding the sinner of the promises of help in the time of trouble. He yielded to the kindly human suggestions of my friend, who did not then know how The Voice was speaking through him words he could not hear. Presently these two were slowly retracing their steps down the hill towards the town, one delivering his Master's message of Good News, the other hungrily applying it to his own starved soul. Soon a part of the story was related, and then my friend knew why he had been led to take his evening walk in an unusual direction at an unusually late hour. It was that he might find this needy sinner. A meal together, a simple prayer, a comfortable bed and a night of silent revealing communion brought the man to the point where the Father "ran to meet him". A few hours later he was sent up to London, where the writer first met him.

Daily contact with him for months has revealed two facts—the power of Christ to transform men so that they be almost unrecognisable spiritually and physically, and the persistency of the Devil in attempts to dispute and challenge this power.

It is because one knows how subtle is this challenging that one must constantly tell forth the evidences which prove the recreating power of Christ's love.

Every day in my own work comes revelation after revelation, in a way no man could plan, that "all things are working together for good to them that love God" (however modern "translations" of the Scriptures may seek to alter that phrase). When men's hearts turn in love to God, the incredible happens: the lost is found; the weak is strengthened; despair vanishes and hope is reborn. There is no other way in human experience by which these effects can be produced. The promises of science, of education, of philosophy, of self-knowledge, self-control, self-improvement, are all futile in the face of those personal temptations which assail the learned and the ignorant alike, which defeat all mental efforts, and overthrow all the bulwarks of so-called culture. Wickedness and weakness are found in those who possess all that money can procure, as well as in those who are said to be driven to sin by poverty and privation. The heart of man is desperately wicked, unlit by the knowledge of the Love of God; and although there be those whose lives are outwardly without reproach, these only know true happiness and the power to bless others when they know and love Christ. Such love transforms not only the giver but the gift, takes the kindly deed and makes it a spiritual enrichment.

A man with whom I shook hands a few days ago and in whose shining eyes I read of a joy and a gratitude beyond words, was a couple of years ago a hopeless physical and moral wreck, suffering the tortures of delirium tremens for the third time, and regarded by the medical man as beyond recovery. In the quiet of a little room in Commercial Road he sought Christ's forgiveness and grace and found them. His power has transformed the whole man and has restored not only moral stability, physical health and the will to live, but has "renewed a right spirit" which now hungers to bless others. Here is transformation to make the sceptic think, for such completed evolution can be achieved in no other way known to us.

Today as I am recording these truths I am involved with another such instance. A man in whose life there has been every possible advantage—excellent parents, every physical comfort, a good physique, first-class health, ample means, the best education—this man yielded to the allurements of the worldly life and became infatuated with persons whose characters were evil, and who soon enticed him into ways of wickedness. His selfishness and baseness brought havoc into the home. His mother died of shame and his father soon followed. Relatives grew tired of his constant public degradation. He sank lower and lower, and when I first saw him he was awaiting trial for complicity in a house-breaking episode during which a woman was nearly killed. He was likely to be judged the guilty person and there seemed to be no way of escape. His remorse was awful to witness. During the waiting period his worst elements found expression in abuse of all who tried to aid him. Then happened the thing which astonished even one who was long experienced in such things. One day upon visiting him and anticipating the usual explosion of wrathful and bitter words, I found him chastened and subdued. His first words were: "Padre, I've talked it all out with Him, and now I feel better."

"With whom?" I asked, for he had given me no sign that the messages I had delivered were even comprehended.

"The Lord Jesus Christ, of Whom you have been telling me," was his clear and welcome reply.

Then followed one of the clearest statements of contrition, repentance and acceptance that I remember hearing. His changed demeanour was the subject of great surprise to all who had to do with him. In a remarkable way evidence was given proving that although he had a hand in the robbery, he was innocent of the more serious charge, since the actual culprit was discovered. He went to gaol, served his sentence, remained true to his declaration of faith in Christ, obtained release in due course, and is today holding a fair position in a London business house, earning the respect of all who know him by his consistent Christian character. Moreover, he is frequently the helper of men whose conduct has led them into prison. Transformed! By what power are these things accomplished?

I want to say most fervently that daily experience of the fulfilment of His great promise causes me to wonder why His disciples do not more generally find the joy of it in their own lives. It can only be, I think, that, like certain sad men who were walking to Emmaus, their eyes are holden that they do not see Him, as He fulfils His word by walking with them. For undoubtedly He is there, as can easily be proved by any converted man or woman who will recognise Him. Unbelief, like wilful disobedience, prevents His "mighty works", as in the days of His flesh. "Faith laughs at impossibilities and cries 'it shall be done!'" —and it happens!

It is high time that organised societies of professing believers faced up to the challenge of the world of today—"Where is thy God?" The Bible is still Truth. The Holy Spirit is still the empowering agent of the Divine will. The Lord Jesus is still the Seeker and Saviour and Transformer of all who will simply and implicitly love and trust Him. The powers of evil are tremendous and subtle, but the Power of Divine Love is irresistible and unalterable. Oh the pity of it that so few Christians are revelling in the full experience of its transforming joy!

"GO YE"

HEARTS there are all void and joyless,
  Which a smile of mine could fill;
There are storms on life's full ocean
  Which a look of mine could still;
There's a life all grey and sunless
  I could flood with beams of light;
There's a soul that I could comfort
  Sitting now in blackest night.

But, alas! I often pass them—
  Wearied hearts with heavy woes
Knowing not the cares that harass,
  Feeling not the cruel blows
Falling thick and fast upon them,
  Swiftly crushing them to earth:
If I knew, I'd try, God knows it,
  Just to bring new hope to birth.

But I do not feel, as He does,
  All the sorrows of the race;
I can scarcely bear my own load
  With a cheerful, smiling face;
Yet I can pass on His warning
  That the world's mad quest is wrong,
That there comes a rude awakening
  For the wicked, proud and strong.

That the sobs and sighs of toilers
  Rises high above the din;
That the cries of little children,
  Paying heavy toll for sin,

Reaches ears that are not heavy,
  Moves a Heart that's full of love;
That a God whose justice fails not
  Sits upon the Throne above.

I can tell of a Redeemer
  Who can touch and make men whole;
I can point them to a Saviour,
  Who can cheer the lonely soul.
I can tell of deep compassion
  Weeping o'er a city's woes,
And a promise of a "desert"
  Which shall "blossom as a rose".

G. F. D.